MW01039333

# VALOR, GUTS, AND LUCK

# VALOR, GUTS, AND LUCK

## A B-17 TAILGUNNER'S SURVIVAL
## STORY DURING WORLD WAR II

**WILLIAM L. SMALLWOOD**

Potomac Books

An imprint of the University of Nebraska Press

This book is dedicated to:

Theresa Jackson, Slayton's number-two daughter, who was at our dinner table one evening telling us about her father's WWII experiences. This sparked my interest in visiting him in Buffalo WY. I found a very bright, honest man with a keen memory, and thanks to Theresa his story will now live on.

John W. Mitchell, my close friend for over sixty years who spent many hard hours teaching me instrument flying in a link trainer, and who, above the hills south of Denver CO, saved my life by, somehow, recovering our airplane from an eleven-cycle flat spin. Now a retired airline pilot and avid WWII reader, I know you will enjoy this story, Mitch.

# TABLE OF CONTENTS

# LIST OF ILLUSTRATIONS

## ACKNOWLEDGMENTS

Six days a week, for four months, at 7:30 a.m. and 1:00 p.m. daily, I was on the telephone with the subject of this story, both of us wearing headsets with microphones, me asking questions and typing while he told the story that you are about to read. During the other hours of the day I had at my fingertips the new and great wonder of the world: the internet, plus nineteen volumes written by scholars of (and participants in) the Eighth Air Force's mission to destroy strategic targets in Germany during World War II. All the while, one of my favorite editor's admonitions—trust but verify—weighed heavily upon my conscience, causing me to constantly do post-interview searches on the internet and in my volumes. I say this hoping the reader can trust that this story has been researched to the best of my ability.

Now for specifics. Abraham Homer, who was a flight engineer in a B-24, parachuted from his crippled airplane the same day the subject crash landed in Germany. Wounded three times, he too had experiences in multiple hospitals, and spent about the same amount of time as the subject in Stalag

Luft IV and VI. His story of being swatted by the goon, Big Stoop, is related in this story, but he kindly spent an hour or more on the telephone giving me other details.

Also a special thanks to Herb Phalen, a volunteer at the Seattle Museum of Flight, who met me at a storage hanger so I could inspect the tail gunner's seat, guns, armor and views in a B-17.

Bob Gilbert, a ball turret gunner on an Eighth Air Force B-17, related stories about gunnery training that my subject had forgotten, and he was kind enough to read a few pages of the manuscript and gave me written comments. Recently, his own book, *The View from the Bottom Up: Growing Up Fast in World War II,* has been published and is available on Amazon.

Ray Busiahn, who escaped on the Black March with the subject, died young and was not available for an interview; however, his son, Tom Busiahn, and daughter, Verna Ness, were both kind enough to tell me everything they had learned about their father assisting the subject, who was near death, escape successfully.

Paul Brauchle, who was the subject's navigator's son that he never got to see, now a retired college professor, has done a lot of research at the German crash site and was very generous in sharing both his observations there and insights into his father's last days before dying of a head wound obtained during their last mission.

There is a vast amount of German POW information on the internet, as well as sources revealing testimony of doctors and others regarding the war crimes of the prison supervisors and guards. Among these I want to name five sites that were most valuable to me: 533rd Bomb Squadron War Diary Index; Bomber Legends by Kelsey McMillan; www.b24.net Second Generation Research; Hell's Angels

303rd Bomb Group; and Shoe Leather Express by Joseph P. O'Donnell.

Finally, I want to thank my oldest son, William M., for his job of critical reading. As usual, his insight made me go back and rewrite some of the material. Thanks again, Bill.

# VALOR, GUTS, AND LUCK

## CHAPTER 1

## Mission Number Thirteen

It was February 22, 1944. The 381st Bomb Group was based at Ridgewell, about thirty miles southeast of Cambridge and eighty miles north-northeast of London, one of thirty-nine bomb groups spread over southeast England. Twenty-year-old staff sergeant Lowell "Slats" Slayton was the tail gunner of B-17 numbered 297474 and one of Fridgen's Pigeons—Lt. Francis Fridgen was the pilot, hence the name of the crew and the subsequent name, Homing Pigeon, that the men gave to their recent replacement airplane. (The overworked ground crew had not yet found time to paint the name on the front fuselage.) It was about seven a.m. when Slats carried the two .50 caliber machine guns for the tail from the small shed where they were kept in wooden boxes. Earlier, as the chief armorer for the bomber, he had wiped the excess oil from Lt. Paul J. Ehmann's two .50s and mounted them in the nose on each side of his navigator's table. Now, after repeating the treatment for his two guns, he was about to raise them up through the tail escape hatch, mount them into position, and attach the two belts that fed them. A damp chill was in the air and some of the other gunners had already mounted their guns and were standing outside the airplane, slapping their arms and making small talk while they waited for their officers and the radioman to come from their pre-mission briefing. It was not the policy of the 381st Bomb Group leaders to admit these men to such briefings. They were to find out where they were going from the pilot after they were airborne.

Slats finished installing his guns. Then, to protect the "family jewels," he spread one piece of his flak jacket under the oversize bicycle seat that he would mount after they were airborne — after a recent accident, when a loaded B-17 failed to maintain flying speed after takeoff and was destroyed in a horrible explosion, the takeoff position policy was changed: all gunners in the back of the airplane were to sit on the floor of the radio room. This did two things: it put the weight of the four men (ball turret gunner, two waist gunners, and the tail gunner) nearer the wing's center of gravity, and moving that weight forward made it easier for the pilot to trim the elevator for the takeoff angle of attack. The other two pieces of the flak jacket were hung below the windows on his right and left, then his parachute, a small chest pack that could be double snapped to the harness he wore, was placed in front and to his left, below the window that looked out to his four o'clock position — a position that would turn out to be a fateful location. When Slats climbed back down out of the tail, S.Sgt. William Reilly, the radio operator, had joined them. He and the others were lamenting the mission number and most admitted that they were worried about unlucky thirteen and what it could mean for them. Then they opened up on S.Sgt. Oliver Gaby, the left waist gunner, reminding him that since he flew as a replacement yesterday, it would not be an unlucky number for him. Gaby, who could exhibit dour moods from time to time, was especially taciturn today and freely expressed his feelings. "I had to bail out over this damned place yesterday because the pilot couldn't land and it sure as hell isn't fair for them to make me fly again today." Everyone, including Slats, agreed with him, but that did not change his mood. And then the conversation changed to a more positive tone.

"You know what this day is, don't you?" one of the men asked, a challenge in his tone.

"Hell, yes," somebody replied. "Anybody who got past the second grade knows that it's George Washington's birthday."

The others chimed in, faking anger that the questioner was some kind of an idiot thinking they would not know the significance of February 22. "Well, let's go do it for George," one commented and, with the exception of Gaby, the rest echoed the same enthusiastic sentiment.

But it was all bravado. Deep within, many of them had gotten the hushed word passed around the crew pipelines that their chances of surviving the twenty-five missions necessary before they could be sent home was 26 percent. Surely none of them had studied probability arithmetic in the 1930s and early 1940s. But they all understood that they faced a one-in-four survival probability. Those were damn poor odds and they knew it.

And they had their own horror-filled experiences to give credence to those statistics. On January 11, on a raid over the Focke-Wulf 190 manufacturing plant near Oschersleben, a small city just west of Magdeburg in north-central Germany, six of the nine airplanes in the 533rd Squadron failed to return and, overall, sixty bombers went down. The antiaircraft artillery that ringed the plant had sent up the heaviest flak that Fridgen's Pigeons had ever seen; the fighter attacks both going and coming from the mission were equally ferocious.

The Pigeons' mission today was a part of the Big Week offensive that the Eighth Air Force planners had unleashed two days earlier, when a Caltech meteorologist on the staff accurately predicted three days of high pressure and clear skies over Germany—following literally months of heavy cloud cover that prohibited accurate bombing of the Eighth staff's highest priority targets. The European invasion was planned for the coming May and the number-one goal was to destroy the German Luftwaffe, thus eliminating threats from the skies over the invading forces. Gen. Jimmy Doolittle, the commanding officer of the Eighth, believed this could be done by two means: first, bombing and destroying the aircraft factories, and second, using escorting fighters to destroy Luftwaffe fighters, primarily single-engine Messerschmitt 109s and Focke-Wulf 190s.

Finally, after many months when the bombers fought their way to and from their targets, there were now hundreds of high-speed P-51 Mustang fighters with long-range tanks that would allow them to escort the bombers to the targets deep into Germany. The Little Friends, as they were called by the bomber crews, would attempt to kill the enemy fighters when they attacked the bombers, and Doolittle, when he took command in January, changed the policy and allowed them to leave the bombers and continue pursuit as the Germans flew back to their bases to refuel.

That morning, on February 22, Lieutenant Fridgen and the other three officers of the crew were driven up to Homing Pigeon, and Slats still remembers studying their faces for a possible clue as to the roughness of the mission. "I didn't seen any signs," he said while remembering the event, "but I think they would have tried to cover up the seriousness of the mission. Fridgen, especially, was a 'we've got a job to do so let's get with it' type of leader. We all had a helluva lot of respect for him, both for his pilot skills and his leadership ability."

Heavy low clouds covered the airfield when the engines were started, and it was hard for Slats and the other gunners sitting on the floor of the radio room to imagine that the sky would be clear over a target in Germany. But maybe it would not be in Germany; maybe they would be going back to those mysterious ground installations in France that an earlier mission had bombed. The waiting, waiting, waiting, and then the slow intermittent taxiing strained their nerves, especially when under "instrument conditions" the takeoffs were spaced at one-minute rather than thirty-second intervals. But as Fridgen shoved the throttles to full power, the airplane, typically overloaded by a thousand pounds with full bomb load and full fuel, began to creep down the runway, gradually picking up enough speed to struggle out of ground effect and into the damp, moisture-laden air. Now that they were airborne and laboring up through the heavy clouds, the men on the floor of the radio room began moving to their positions. S.Sgt. Garrett Bartle took his position in the ball turret that hung below the belly of the airplane. S.Sgt. Walter Abernathy moved to his position at the right waist of the fuselage—his position in this new airplane was slightly forward of the waist gunner's position on the left side, a refinement that virtually eliminated the problem of the two gunners colliding with each other as they manned their single .50s out the windows of the waist. Then they all noted that Staff Sergeant Gaby, who was to man the left waist position, did not stand up when he got to his position. Instead, adding emphasis to his upset feelings about having to fly so soon after his parachute escape the day before, he sat defiantly on the floor and did not move as Slats stepped beside him and began to crawl around the tail wheel to his position. There, he knelt, put his knees on the two leather-lined rubber pads mounted in the floor, and settled on to his oversize bicycle seat. It was an uncomfortable position but, as he recalled later, "being young I was never bothered by cramps even after an eight-hour mission. In fact, I liked the isolation of the tail; I liked being off by myself. And, yeah, it was a rough place to ride, especially in turbulence when the tail moved more than any other part of the airplane. But none of that bothered me; I never once even got close to being air sick."

Then Fridgen, who was adamant about radio discipline and unnecessary chatter, came on the intercom, called for a crew check, and announced the mission: Oschersleben. He did not comment further, but he did not need to. They had gone there January 11 and seen sixty of their squadron friends and roommates fall out of the sky, and their airplane had been so badly damaged that it had to be replaced. Of course, under Fridgen's stern hand, there was no rebuttal, no 'here we go again'-type comments. And, according to Slats's memory, he began to wonder about the number thirteen and whether it was truly an unlucky number. But then his strong conscience took over and he forced such thoughts from his mind. He had never believed that he would be killed, and while not a praying man at the time, the inner strength of his character took over – a character hardened by an impoverished childhood in the Great Depression. He was going to do the two things that he had been trained to do. He was going to keep his head moving to spot enemy fighters before they were close enough to do damage with their 20mm exploding shells, and he was going to fire his twin .50s in short bursts and at the angles he had been trained to use. The number thirteen was just a number; let somebody else think about superstitious witchcraft.

But the morning was not going right, and the crew in the rear of the airplane sensed it. There was too much maneuvering, and with little results. Normally, after an hour or so, they would have joined others in their squadron and their group and would be flying in a tight formation. But, looking out, Slats and the others saw only one other B-17 with the white triangle and the letter "L" in it — another airplane from the 381st Group. Finally, Fridgen saw a formation at their two o'clock position and he and the bomber on his wing eased over and edged into the left side of that formation. Lieutenant Ehmann then confirmed that they were on the proper course that was briefed. (To confuse the opposition one or more courses might be flown before a course was selected to the target.) What Fridgen did not know because of radio silence was that other members of his squadron and group had either aborted the mission or joined another group.

Soon, Lt. Ehmann announced that they were over the Channel, which meant that each gun was to be test fired so any malfunctions could be detected and repaired. In the tail that eventuality never concerned Slats because as chief armorer, he supervised the maintenance of all the guns and made certain that his strict standards were always observed. Still, the short chatter of the guns broke the monotony and set the adrenaline flowing. In minutes they would be over hostile territory where both flak and enemy fighters could appear at any moment. But as they droned on, an hour, perhaps more, passed without them seeing flak or fighters. Occasionally they would look up to check if the escort fighters were covering them, but Slats has no memory of seeing any of them. What he does remember is the call somebody eventually made that a twin-engine ME-210 was at their nine-thirty position, level. (It was more likely a BF-110 or BF-410, but from a distance they looked the same. Because they were manufactured by Messerschmitt, crews used the ME designation rather than the correct BF prefix.) He looked right, then leaned forward to where he could see the ten o'clock position, but no 210 was in sight. Thinking that there could be another one out there he immediately started scanning all the sky that was visible. And then it happened: "It sounded like a freight train had hit us, and the noise and rush of cold air was like a tornado." Then he realized what had happened. One of the ninety-pound, eight-inch mortar rockets from the 210 had hit the fuselage behind him and passed within inches of his back, exiting his compartment at his left front and creating a hole eighteen inches wide. Slats stared at the gaping hole, not realizing that it was where his parachute had been. Then the chill of the air started freezing him, and before he could comprehend that the rocket had taken out his communications, his electrical suit, and his oxygen supply, he slumped over the armor plate in front of him, unconscious from anoxia.

Meanwhile Fridgen was frantically calling him to find out what had happened—Abernathy had informed him about the rocket hole and was feeling relief that it did not explode: it had a timed fuse that often exploded before or after passing through a bomber. Then Fridgen ordered Abernathy to go back and check on Slayton and assess the damage. Abernathy took a walk-around oxygen bottle, crawled beside the tail wheel, and saw Slayton slumped over his armor plate. "He looks okay—I don't think it hit him," he said to Fridgen, "but he's slumped over his armor. The rocket must have taken out all his connections—also blew out his chute. But the fuselage looks okay except there's a big hole where it exited." Fridgen then had to make a quick decision. He knew that at his present altitude of 24,000 feet Slayton only had minutes to live without oxygen—not to mention the 50-below-zero air blowing over him that would soon freeze his body. But, if he dove down, which he would have to do immediately in order to save Slayton, he would be leaving the safety of the formation and subjecting the rest of the crew to the swarms of marauding fighters that always ganged up on single bombers. Was saving one life worth the risk of the nine other lives? We will never know exactly how Fridgen arrived at his agonizing decision. What we do know is that he immediately, with all his strength and perhaps with the help of copilot Lt. David Waller, pushed the yoke far forward and Homing Pigeon went into a screaming power dive.

## CHAPTER 2

## Little Slats

Lowell Slayton was born in Valley City, North Dakota, on October 30, 1923. He was the sixth and last child of Iver and Christine. Iver was born in 1895 in Norway, but he never talked about his parents; no one in his family even knew if he had brothers or sisters, and he never explained how he got to the United States. The only clue anybody had was that his English was perfect, which indicated that he had learned the language when he was small. He was a big man, probably more than six feet in height, and was lean and trim throughout his life.

Christine was born on May 20, 1897, in the northeastern Iowa town of Stacyville to a German family with the sur-name of Vinkle, later changed to Winkle. There were nine girls—she was the fifth and was probably the runt of the litter, for she was only four-foot-ten as an adult. Both she and Iver were working on the harvest circuit in 1909 when they met and married. In those times, before combines were invented, grain had to be threshed, which was a multistep process that no farmer could accomplish by himself. The problem was solved by itinerant workers—the men working in the fields and the women working in the kitchens helping with the cooking that had to be done to feed the hungry laborers.

The Slayton family, in order of birth, included Einer (1912), Hazel (1914), Donald (1917), Willard (1919), James (1921), and Lowell. All of the boys except Lowell were tall like their father. He took after his mother, although he was told that at birth he was a "blue baby" and that this temporary defect may have both stunted his growth and later delayed his teenage growth spurt. He was only five feet tall when he graduated from high school—the smallest boy in his class. (We will never know for sure, but a doctor friend of the author suggested that it could have been VSD, which is a condition when the partition between the two heart ventricles has not completely formed at birth—during the early fetal stages there is no partition between them. This opening usually grows shut during the first few months after birth, but it creates a mild, but temporary oxygen deprivation that can cause a bluish tint of the skin.)

Iver and Christine moved their family to an apartment in Fargo when Lowell was four, and Iver found a job with a painting contractor. However, he developed a problem that caused his family to suffer, especially after the Great Depression hit in 1929. He loved to play cards and gamble, and after each payday, he would find a poker table before he came home. And when he did get home and went to sleep, Christine would get up and search his pockets, always hoping that there would be enough to buy food for the family the upcoming week. Little Slats—his older brother Jimmy was called "Slats" and Lowell, hating his name, asked to be called the diminutive form—remembers the sad looks on his mother's face when there was little or no money available to feed the eight of them. However, Einer and Hazel, and then Don and

Willard—he also hated his name and wanted to be called Bill—started working at odd jobs at an early age and were able to bring home to mom enough to keep the family from going hungry. "It was a good thing people didn't like liver in those days," Slats said while talking about his growing up years. "The butcher shops couldn't sell it so they gave it away. There was a shop down the street and the guy liked my mother, so believe me, we grew up not only eating a lot of it but liking it."

Growing up, clothes were always an embarrassing problem because all Little Slats ever got were the hand-me-downs. He never ever wore overalls like most of the farm boys of the period, but in a location where temperatures of thirty to forty below were common during the long winters, heavy cotton corduroys were the mainstay in the trouser department—although he remembers that by the time they were fitted to his smaller frame, the ridges of the corduroy were mostly worn off. And shoes? Unlike many of the boys whose parents ordered high-top boots with a knife pocket on the side from Sears, Roebuck or "Monkey Ward" (as the Montgomery Ward catalog was known), Slats is adamant that he never once wore a single pair of leather shoes, even up to the time he left for service at age of eighteen.

However, one Christmas he did receive a special gift that allowed him to mingle with some of the more affluent kids in the neighborhood. Einer and Hazel pooled their money and bought him a sled. He still smiles when he tells of the wonderful weekend days when he would pull it about a block north of their home and ride it down the steep bank of the Red River, then across the ice to the town of Moorhead, Minnesota. He thinks he was eight when they did that, and probably no gift during his entire life was more appreciated.

Little Slats was probably ten or eleven when he earned his first money for the family. The Eighth Street Shoe Repair Shop was in their neighborhood, and after pestering the owner it was agreed that he could come in and shine the repaired shoes for five cents a pair. (The reason the owner was reluctant was because of a shoeshine "boy" who had a stand in the neighborhood; it was the way he made a living for his family.) Slats can remember making as much as ten cents on some afternoons after school, and the big treat was when the customer gave him a penny tip. His mother agreed that this was his money to spend and in those days there were many varieties of penny sweet treats that could be purchased. "Only someone who grew up in those times can ever have an appreciation for what a penny could buy."

Boys in those days often got into fist fights that degraded into wrestling matches and ended when one got his shoulders pinned and muttered the words, "I give up." For a number of years Little Slats did not have to worry about such events because of the threat from his protective older brothers. But then one day it happened: a boy in his neighborhood attacked him and bloodied his nose. Little Slats got home just as his brothers arrived—both Don and Jimmy had been caddying at the Fargo Country Club—and he went to them, crying and with his nose still bleeding. However, they refused to go back out with him and find his assailant. Instead, they gave him a combination pep talk and berating speech, insisting that it was time for him to grow up, time for him, despite his small size, to go find that guy and go after him like a tiger. Taking their words to heart, that is exactly what he did. The next time he saw the one who had hurt him, "I knocked the living daylights out of that kid, and I was so happy when I went home I could hardly stand it."

And then he admitted, "Yes, that incident probably started to build a bit of a pugnacious attitude that, along with other events in my young life, helped me when things got tough."

Slats's young life slowly began to fall into a four-dimensional routine.

First, there were the home responsibilities. His mother inherited her Germanic organizational imperatives and so she had a rigid weekly routine. On Mondays she would wash. On Tuesdays she would sprinkle the clothes. On Wednesdays she would iron. On Thursdays she baked. On Fridays she mended kids' clothes and darned socks. Then on Saturdays Jimmy and Little Slats came into the picture. That was the day the house had to be cleaned and, today, unless one has seen German housewives at work cleaning their homes in modern times, she could have been called a cleanliness fanatic. They swept and they mopped and they dusted, they washed windows and, when the snow melted and the temperatures moderated, they took the carpets outside, hung them on the clothesline, and beat them with paddle-like tools called "carpet beaters." They also had daily chores. Mother did all the cooking for their evening meal, but that was the end of her workday. Jimmy and Little Slats had to take over from there. They carried the dishes to the sink, scraped them clean (which was not much of a task because of their mother's constant admonition to "take what you want but eat what you take"), then every evening they would take turns washing and drying. And as Slats later related, one argument with Jimmy revealed an early character trait. "He kept saying that it was his turn to dry and my turn to wash, but I argued strongly that he was wrong because my memory never failed. After mom heard this for a while, she turned to Jimmy and said, 'You might as well give up because Little Slats is always right.' She really liked Jimmy and always believed him even when he was lying—which he did a lot, but when she said that, it really got my attention and made

*Little Slats*

me believe, despite a strong inferiority complex I had then, that my voice was respected."

The second dimension in his life was school. Unlike his three oldest brothers, who did not even think of attending high school before moving into the work force, Jimmy and Little Slats did go on after their eighth grade graduation and attend Roosevelt High School. But Jimmy was not serious and often "ditched" school to play pool or snooker—the latter a pool-like game but with smaller balls, much smaller pockets, and played on a larger table. And soon after starting the tenth grade he quit, telling his mother that "I can't stand it because Little Slats is always making me look bad."

There may have been some justification in his older brother's frustration because Little Slats was an excellent student who went on to graduate from high school in three and a half years. His graduation class had forty-four students and in those years it was not uncommon for a high school to have two ceremonies, one in January and a second in May. Also, academically, he graduated as the number one boy in his class. He was not accorded the term "honors graduate" because he had not participated in any school activities that honor students were expected to. And that embarrassment was directly related to the third dimension of his life.

Like all his siblings, Little Slats had to work and bring money home so the family could eat. As mentioned earlier, he started out shining shoes. Then he became what was called a "paper boy" by delivering the *St. Paul Pioneer Press* to people's homes. Then during the summer months, his older brothers got him on as a caddy at Fargo Country Club, where he earned fifty cents for carrying the clubs for eighteen holes—later in his high school years the pay was raised to sixty-five cents. Then, as soon as he turned six-teen and could get a driver's license, he got a job with the Brixton News Service.

Neil Brixton had the business delivering magazines and *The New York Sunday News* to retail outlets in Fargo, West Fargo, and Moorhead, across the Red River. When Slats applied for a job, he was told to take a driving test. With Brix-ton watching him closely as he drove away and with the admo-nition ringing in ears not to put a dent in the truck, Slats drove to the university, then came back and stopped. When Little Slats was hired, he learned why Brixton was so concerned about a driver. Brixton told him the story of how he had gone to visit friends, parked in their driveway, then went inside. The front door of the house happened to be open, and with-out anybody observing his friends' baby, he crawled outside and ended up behind one of the rear wheels of Brixton's truck. Later, as he backed out of the driveway he felt a bump and it was the child. He had run over and killed the child and even at the time he hired Little Slats, he hated to drive, warned Lit-tle Slats never to back up farther than he had to, and when they were working together, the new hire did all of the driving.

The Brixton News job was a good one—Slats searched his memory and thinks it earned him about five dollars a week. But it took a lot of time. The biggest problem was that his services were needed every Monday afternoon in addition to his after-school, Saturday, and Sunday work, and Little Slats had to get permission from his high school principal to miss half a day of school on Mondays. The fact that he was an "A" student and needed the money probably influenced the administrator's decision to give his permission. Almost seventy years later, Slats still remembers three of the best-selling magazines: *Liberty* magazine, *True Story*, and *Better Homes and Gardens*. He also remembers the work that was necessary to get the two thousand copies of *The New York Sunday News* ready for the outlets. "Neil and I had to go to the depot where the papers arrived in three sections that we had to stuff together. As I recall, it was the news section, the funnies—they were colored even then, and the sports section. We spent hours stuffing these together and it was the hardest work I had to do on that job." And even with this workload, he was still able to maintain his outstanding academic record—he finished all his homework in study hall.

However, the Brixton News job did not last for the rest of his school career, and Slats explains why: "Neil hired a guy to help me that I did not like, and soon it was impossible to work with him. Finally, I quit the weekly job and, because Neil liked to have Sundays off to be with his family, I agreed to continue to work Sundays for him." When Little Slats left that job, he was immediately hired by Spangler's IGA market as the afternoon delivery boy. "Mr. Spangler was a wonderful man and I really enjoyed working for him. I've forgotten what he paid, but for the time it was good pay and it really helped my mother, especially after all of my older brothers and sister except Jimmy were gone from home—and Jimmy, who was hoping to be a golf pro like brother Don, who had landed that job at the Lewistown, Montana, Golf Club, contributed little or nothing. But, I have to tell you one story I'll never forget. I was taking this box of groceries up to the back door of this house and a young good-looking woman, dressed only in a slip, came to the door and said, 'Aren't you going to come in and bring the groceries?' The way she said it implied that she had something else in mind and I'm sure my face turned as red as my hair because I was really embarrassed. I quickly handed her the box and got out of there fast, but when I told Mr. Spangler, he smiled and said, 'You should have stuck around awhile and found out what she had in mind.' I may have laughed, but the point is, I was extremely shy around girls even when I was eighteen, which was probably my age when that happened. There was no way I could have stuck around at that time."

Now to the fourth dimension: recreation. Yes, Slats—the "Little" was dropped when Jimmy quit high school—found time from his busy schedule for some recreation. One of the favorite hangouts for many of the young men was the Grand Recreation, an establishment with pool tables equipped with Kelly strings—strings above the tables where, with a pool cue, one could reach up and slide numbers to a score-keeping position for the gambling game called Kelly Pool (also known as pea pool). Then there were the billiard tables where both three-cushion and carom billiards were played. Finally, there were the big snooker tables with their small balls and narrow pockets. Both Jimmy and Slats loved playing snooker and each had their special talents for different shots.

They also played ice hockey together but, again, Slats was to embarrass his older brother. Said Slats, "Jimmy got mad because I had so much speed I could come up from behind him and steal his puck. It was a fast and tough game—I learned to do clean clips right away. I just loved ice hockey." (A clean clip occurred when a player used his shoulder to strike his opponent's shoulder and send him off into another direction. A dirty clip, a serious foul, was hitting an opponent's lower back, which could cause serious injury.)

But it was at the Fargo Arena that Slats's talent grew and blossomed. This was the roller rink for the city, where mostly young people rented wood-wheeled roller skates and, to the beat of the ever present recorded music emanating from a speaker system, each skater did his or her thing. In those years it was difficult for a boy to meet a girl and hold hands with her, but at the Fargo Arena a boy could pair up with a girl, take her left hand in his left hand, then wrap his right arm around her waist, and away they would go, matching the rhythm of the music with their skate strokes. Slats started skating there even before going to high school and got very good, at least at individual skating—he didn't skate with girls because of his shyness. However, when he got into high school, his skill was so noticeable that the owner would admit him free of charge if he would spend some of his time teaching others to skate.

And that is how Cliff Myhra got his start.

Cliff was Slats's classmate and one of his close buddies—the other was Don Munson, another classmate. Cliff did not know how to roller skate, and Slats took it upon himself to correct that deficiency. "And did I ever do a good job. In six months nobody could touch him." What Slats meant by that statement is that six months after he started skating, Cliff was doing the most fantastic twirling and other showmanship maneuvering that anybody had ever seen. Of course Slats reveled in the challenge of performing show-stopping maneuvers with Cliff, and by the time they were seniors, an older admirer named Leonard Johnson drove them down to a famous rink in St. Paul, Minnesota. There they dazzled the skating crowd with their two-step routine and their twirling, and were invited back for an exhibition. Johnson drove them again and this time, they did a spectacular number where Slats locked his legs around Cliff's neck, then stretched out with his hands down near the floor while Cliff did a series of rapid twirls. Slats now says, modestly, that "we put on a pretty good show and they really applauded us. That made us feel good."

But something else happened during their senior year that had the opposite effect. It was a little more than a month after Slats turned eighteen, and also a month before he was to graduate. It was a Sunday and he was in the Eighth Street Cigar store checking on sales of *The New York Sunday News* when the proprietor told him that the Japanese had attacked Pearl Harbor in Hawaii. "I laughed when I heard that and said, 'Nobody is going to do that.'" Slats then drove to Moorhead and when he checked his first newsstand, there was already a copy of the *Fargo Forum* with a headline announcing the attack. Soon all Americans were reading and listening to the radio for details. However, Americans didn't learn the complete story until four years later: on Sunday morning, December 7, 1941, Japanese torpedo bombers destroyed or disabled America's entire Pacific battleship fleet—ships that were anchored and lined up in a perfect row for the Japanese bombers.

The next morning all the students were told to gather in the assembly room, and there they listened to a radio on stage that broadcast President Roosevelt's "Day of Infamy" speech—a speech Slats claims to remember vividly even now. Of course he knew the consequences as soon as he heard it. He, along with millions of other young American men who were listening to the President's speech, were just months away from a war in which many of them would be fighting for their lives.

## CHAPTER 3

## I Want You!

Every man and woman old enough to remember World War II will also remember the big poster that was in every railroad train depot in America. It showed the face of a stern-looking Uncle Sam with his long, boney right index finger pointing and with a message below him in big type saying "I want you!" Beneath that, most of the posters added a line in smaller type: "For U.S. Army." It is probably not the exact message of those posters that made them so memorable, but the fact that no matter where you went or from what angle you saw the poster, Uncle Sam's finger was always pointing at you. In fact, it was a common sight in railroad stations to see kids walking from side to side, giggling and pointing their fingers back at the poster. They were learning that there was no way they could escape that finger.

And that was the message the artist wanted every young man to understand. No matter how frightened he was of going into service in those years, there was no way of escaping or ducking the responsibility. If you were the right age and physically qualified, you were going, period—unless, of course, the government gave you some "critical skill" deferment.

Slats Slayton clearly remembers the kinds of thoughts both he and his close friends had at the time. He and Don Munson knew that it was inevitable and thought, "If that is what we have to do, that is what we will do." Not Cliff Myhra. "He was scared to death, claimed that he was not a fighter, and knew that he would be killed. And he was, almost as soon as he got to France."

After graduation in January, Slats received a notice from the draft board indicating that he was designated 1-A—prime material for the U.S. Army. However, he did not want to join the U.S. Army, at least in what was known as the "regular" army. Like most young men his age, he had grown up watching the newsreels and seeing Charles Lindbergh, Jimmy Doolittle, and other famous flyers being idolized by their fans. And there were Jimmy Allen and Captain Midnight in the late afternoon radio serials that were so popular with boys in those days. In short, aviation had glamour and of the four service anthems that were sung in every school in the nation, the "Off we go into the wild blue yonder" line was, by far, the most stimulating and motivational. So, like thousands of others, Slats wanted to spend his service days in that wild blue yonder; he wanted to enlist in the U.S. Army Air Force (AAF).

And so did two of his brothers, Don and Bill—Einer had physical problems because of an earlier ruptured appendix and Jimmy was disqualified because of a problem with his kidneys. So, when the local draft board notified Slats that he was about to receive his call-up notice, he enlisted in the AAF. It was October 8, 1942—twenty-two days before his nineteenth birthday. Both Don and Bill had already enlisted—Don was in aviation mechanics school and Bill in radio school learning to be a high-speed operator.

*I Want You!*

Of course there were other good reasons why Don and Bill and Slats and so many other young men wanted to get into the AAF rather than the regular army. When they were thinking about their options in 1942, it had only been twenty-four years since the Great War—which now came to be called World War I. In many towns and cities men could be observed who were missing limbs and fingers or wearing dark green glasses because their eyes had been injured in poisonous gas attacks. They had been the ones firing the rifles and machine guns in that war and they elicited no envious looks. And while high-scoring fighter aces like Captain Eddie Rickenbacker were popular speakers and were lauded nationwide, those who had fought in the trenches, if they could even be made to discuss their wartime experiences, had no tales of glamour to tell. And then there were books like the bestseller *All Quiet on the Western Front*, so morbidly realistic that it absolutely destroyed all fantasies a reader might have that infantry fighting could be exciting and glamorous. In short, Don and Bill and Slats also wanted to avoid the brutality and hazards of ground combat.

From the local recruiting station, Slats was given a ticket to Minneapolis where a bus took him out to Fort Snelling. There he took the physical during which he was measured twice to be certain that his height was, indeed, five feet two inches, the minimum height to be accepted. Luckily, his delayed growth spurt was kicking in, for he had already grown two inches since graduation. The first night he slept in a barracks cot and admits that it was not only the loneliest night of his young life but that he felt so homesick that he cried.

Then, after the routine series of "shots"—immunizations that all had to endure, and after being outfitted with the complete AAF uniforms, underclothing, socks, shoes, toiletries, and barracks bag to store them in, he shipped his civilian clothes home. After that, he was allowed to visit an aunt in Minneapolis before he boarded a train for St. Louis and the basic training base at Jefferson Barracks.

Unlike many World War II veterans who complained about their harsh treatment in basic training, Slats has good memories of the experience. Yes, there were unpleasant moments, like when a masochistic captain made them wear their overcoats while standing in a formation, causing a number of them to pass out from the heat. But he was lucky enough to have a drill sergeant he described as a nice man, and who, when volunteers were needed to assist with the close-order drill, picked Slats to do the job. "It was really fun to march the men, separate them into groups going opposite directions, then bring them back together again, all while they were chanting refrains to match their steps, like 'the coffee ... that they ... gave us ... they say ... is mighty fine ... it's good ... for cuts and bruises ... and tastes ... like iodine.' The drill sergeant told me that I was pretty damn good, and maybe I was."

Slats also excelled in his treks through the obstacle course, taking great pride in beating everyone else through it. Undoubtedly, these achievements, along with his successful drill instructor experiences, had to be important factors in building some confidence that he totally lacked before he enlisted.

But, he did have some problems during basic training. They were living in tents, five of them sleeping on what were called "camp cots"—cots that were just canvas suspended from a wooden frame that could be folded. One day, four of the men got notice that they were to report at four o'clock the next morning for KP duty—duty in the dining or "mess" hall doing a variety of kitchen jobs. The night before, they bet Slats money that he wouldn't wake up at reveille—he was a sound sleeper and they had been awakening him. Sure enough, he overslept, reported to the orderly room an hour late for drill, and was given a "royal chewing" before he was released to go to the drill field.

Then, unbeknown to him, two skating friends (twins) from Moorhead came to St. Louis as part of the cast of *The Ice Follies*, in which they were to do a special performance. Learning that Slats was there, they came out to JB—no one called it Jefferson Barracks—met with Slats's commander, gave him complimentary tickets for their show, then asked if their good friend could come into town for a few days. "Of course, we'll give him a three-day pass," was his immediate reply. Then, Slats was called to the orderly room, given his pass, and he rode off with the twins. "We stayed in the Chase Hotel, the swankiest hotel in town, and one of the owners, a Mr. Johnson, took us out for dinner at least one of those nights. That was a new experience for this poor boy, also an unforgettable one."

When Slats came back and joined his group in the tent, "they were staring daggers at me" because they had just found that all four of them had to report for KP again the next day. "How do you manage so much pull?" one of them asked angrily. But then the story gets worse—or better, depending on the perspective.

One day, just as an escort was taking him to the post where he would stand guard duty, a runner from the orderly room came with another man to take his place and said, "You've got a phone call in the orderly room." When Slats got there, a clerk dialed a number and handed the phone to Slats. The voice told Slats who he was, a captain somebody, and Slats replied that he did not know the person. Then the voice asked, "Did you have a bookkeeping instructor in high school by the name of Osman?"

Slats replied in the affirmative, then the voice said, "This is Captain Osman, you were the best student I had while I was teaching at Roosevelt, and now I'm here in St. Louis in the Induction Center. How would you like to get away from that camp and spend three days with me?"

Slats replied that there was no way they were going to turn him loose for three days—he doesn't remember if he mentioned the earlier three-day pass. Captain Osman just scoffed. "Don't worry about it," he said. "I'll call your commanding officer."

So Slats got another three-day pass, and when his tent-mates found out about it, they almost went berserk. "Who do you know? What kind of a suck-ass are you?" they ranted. "It's just plain chickenshit for us to be here pulling KP and you getting all these passes." That is part of the dialogue Slats thinks he remembers, but they could have said more and even made some threats. Regardless, Slats shrugs off their ravings. "I didn't have anything to do with it so I had no reason to worry about it. It was their problem, not mine. But, I'm surprised, looking back, that they didn't kick the hell out of me."

Slats enjoyed the three days with his old high school teacher who was lonely in the city without his family. And while they visited and talked old times, Osman made a special effort to convince Slats that he had to get over his inferiority complex. He tried to convince his former student that with his ability, both mental and physical, he should apply for pilot training, or at least for Officer Candidate School (OCS). Slats demurred, saying that he was too young and inexperienced to be ordering other men around, and as for pilot training, he said he had no interest in trying to learn how to fly. According to Slats's memory of that three-day weekend, his former teacher's efforts had no real effect. "I still felt I was an inferior person and way too immature to take on such responsibilities."

Then, somewhere about this time, he had his second embarrassing moment—earlier he had forgotten to salute an officer and received a "royal chewing out." This time he was standing at attention in a formation when a first lieutenant came up to him, moved his face inches from Slats, and growled, "Private Slayton, next time I want you to stand a little closer to your razor."

Slats muttered a meek reply: "Sir, I have never shaved before."

The lieutenant probably replied, but his words are lost in history. Almost seventy years later Slats remembers thinking, "I just had a little red peach fuzz on my face, but I guessed I'd better use that razor and Palmolive soap they gave me." And so he shaved for the first time.

The six weeks of basic training were winding down and somehow—Slats does not remember the details—he was given a chance to list his preferences for the AAF job he would assume, and he got his first choice. He wanted to be a gunner and he received orders to report for gunnery training at Las Vegas Army Airfield—the site of the present international airport.

Along with others headed west he boarded a troop train in St. Louis—he thinks there were about fifty men who did not make it because of flu and other respiratory diseases that were prevalent—his four tent mates were all sick and could not travel. When they arrived in Las Vegas, he remembers a huge dust storm heading toward them, and then, when he got into his barracks, the wind blew dust under the doors and through gaps in the windows, and it was a terrible mess that greeted him after waking up the first morning. After they cleaned the barracks, they were instructed by a sergeant on how to make a bed "Army style." They had real beds with mattresses in this barracks and Slats immediately claimed a top bunk—a practice he would always follow while he was in service. As for the bed making, he remembers how easy it was to make "hospital corners," and how difficult to get the blanket so tight that a dime would flip when dropped on it.

Slats loved the gunnery training. First, there was the skeet shooting from the ground, then while riding in the back of a truck. Then there was a series of familiarization exercises with the .50 caliber machine gun that he would be manning. They took one apart, put it back together, then did the same thing while blindfolded and with gloves on, and this was repeated until the procedures were so routine they did not have to think, but did them automatically. There was also aircraft recognition training: images were flashed on a screen and the men instantly had to identify both enemy and friendly fighters. Finally, while standing in the backseat of an AT-6 trainer, they fired at big banners being towed by another airplane. The first time Slats did this he forgot to pull his goggles down and failed miserably because his eyes were watering so badly. Each trainee had different colored bullets in his gun belt and the next time Slats went up, everybody wanted to know who was shooting the blue bullets. Turned out that it was Slats and he literally pulverized the target. And when the six weeks were up, they were given their final training score and Slats had a 94.3; Ray Veth, a good friend from Ohio, had a 94.4; and they were beaten only by a Captain Lee who was taking the training so he could start a gunnery school in Kingman, Arizona. Then the top ten enlisted graduates were offered a special prize: attendance at OCS—which Slats turned down, telling his commanding officer that he just did not feel like he was mature enough or self-confident enough to be ordering other men around.

Las Vegas at that time had two big casinos, the Last Frontier and El Rancho Vegas, and when his class graduated two days after Christmas, the Last Frontier rewarded them with a big celebratory dinner. Practically all of the gunners—they could call themselves that now—partook generously of the free beer, but Slats abstained. "They really gave me a hard time about it but I didn't want to emulate anybody, I just wanted to be myself; I had never drunk liquor and I couldn't see any sense in starting now."

After that dinner, a bunch of hung-over gunners boarded a troop train for their destination: Lowry Field (later known as Lowry Air Force Base) in Denver, Colorado. They arrived the night of December 31—New Year's Eve, were placed in permanent brick barracks, and were immediately enrolled in an advanced course for gunners called the armament school. January 1, 1943, was no holiday, because America was at war with the Axis—Germany, Italy, and Japan—and it was by no means certain who would win. Everything was on an emergency basis and there were almost no priorities higher than getting men trained and sent to the fronts where they could enter battle with the enemy. At least two of the enemies were extremely formidable. The Germans were skilled, proud warriors, and in a number of ways had weapons that were technologically superior. The Japanese were not just dedicated warriors but fanatical in their fervor—Bushido, their unique military code, would never allow them to surrender even when they were overwhelmed by men and machines. Neither Slats nor any of the gunners knew who they would eventually be fighting. But they were certain that it would be a vicious and determined enemy.

The armament school included a four-week curriculum, but Slats was not destined to finish with his classmates. He thinks it might have been after he had been in school for a week, after he received his second allotment of new uniforms—he was in his growth spurt now and was putting on about an inch a month—when he was called to the orderly room. There, he was told that his mother was extremely ill and that he was to be granted emergency leave so he could see her in the hospital—she was not expected to live and Hazel, his sister, could not leave her children and had somehow convinced the AAF to release Slats to attend his mother's last days.

He immediately left for Fargo, went to his mother's side at the hospital, and learned that she was suffering from severe anemia. However, by the time he arrived, she had been given a number of transfusions and the doctors now believed that she would likely survive. He no longer remembers how long he stayed with her but is fairly certain it was nearly a month before she was able to return to her apartment. Then he was off to Denver and, while living and attending classes with an entirely new group of trainees, he completed the school. After graduation he was promoted to "buck" sergeant— a three striper—and with 123 of the other graduates was shipped by troop train to Godman Army Airfield outside Fort Knox, Kentucky.

"When we got there, it was like arriving at the Air Force Country Club," Slats said. "The quarters were great, the food was great—and at this time my appetite was literally insatiable—I just could not get enough to eat. And I never did figure out why they sent us there unless it was just to hold us in place until there were enough airplanes for the gunners that were ready. And, yeah, we had a few B-25s on the base—maybe ten or eleven—but there was no way they were going to give us the four-hours-a-month flying time we now needed to draw flight pay."

Still, Slats eventually found a way to get that pay. At a barber shop, one of the patrons lying in a barber chair with a towel around his face suddenly got up, pulled off the towel, and said, "Slayton, I thought that was your voice I heard. What in the hell are you doing here?"

Instantly Slats recognized a good friend who was a half year behind him at Roosevelt High School. Slats explained that he had just graduated from armament training and other than that he had no idea why he was at Godman, unless it was to kill time until they could assign him to a crew. Then he explained that he was frustrated because there was no way he could get his four hours of flight time in so he could collect his flight pay.

His friend, Morris Johnson, laid back down in the chair to get the shave that he had come in for, and when he sat back up, he winked at Slats and said something to the effect of, "No worries, old friend. I'm one of the tech sergeant pilots of both the L-4 [a modified Piper Cub] and the L-5 [a two-seat tandem version of a civilian Stinson]. I'll take care of my old buddy."

Both the L-4 and L-5 were liaison aircraft, used primarily for artillery spotting but also for dropping markers to guide fighters in to strafe enemy targets. (One version of the L-5 could carry a stretcher and was also used as an aerial ambulance.) Sometime after their meeting, Slats crawled in the backseat of an L-5 and Johnson took him on two two-hour sight-seeing tours of the countryside. On the first trip, Johnson took him down to fifty feet, then flew him around the Churchill Downs racetrack where the Kentucky Derby is run. "Now you can say you've been there," Johnson told Slats over the intercom. On the next flight they were out in the country when they saw a good-looking young woman standing out in front of a gas station. "He went down and flew right over the top of her." Then he said, "She didn't move; I'll make her move the next time." He then dove again, and as they came down at her, Slats was sure he was going to hit her. Then he pulled up, circled, and they could see that she was lying on the ground. Later, when they landed, a loudspeaker announced, "Technical Sergeant Morris Johnson report to the orderly room immediately." He did and was grounded. "And that was the last time I saw him," said Slats. "I heard later that he was sent to Italy, was hit by the Germans, never got out of his plane, and was killed either in the air or in the crash."

Slats did get his four hours in and also two rides in one of the B-25s, which was "the noisiest airplane I was ever in." Then he got a special assignment: he was put on KP duty, but as the KP supervisor whose only job was to assign the other men to various mess hall chores. But, after three days, he was relieved when the mess hall sergeant said, "I'm relieving you of your duty because I can't afford to keep you around any longer; you eat too much." Slats laughed when telling this, then said, "Whatever being a blue baby did to my growth curve, it sure went away fast. By this time I was literally eating like a hog and I had grown seven inches just in the months I had been in service. I was now five feet, nine inches tall and had to get another set of uniforms."

Soon Slats and the other 123 boarded a troop train again and were taken on a two- or three-day cross-country trip to Salt Lake City, Utah, to what was called a redistribution center. There, he learned that he had no official duties until he was assigned to a bomber crew, so "for several days I laid in the sack, read, and just killed time." Then he got his orders: he was to report to Alexandria Army Air Field outside Alexandria, Louisiana. His assignment was to a B-17 bomber crew.

*I Want You!*

## CHAPTER 4

## The New Crew

It was called combat replacement crew training, a name that speaks for itself. Slats and those he was to meet when he arrived at Alex—nobody ever uttered the full name, Alexandria—were destined to fly in the vacant formation slots, primarily in Europe, where hundreds of their kind were being blown out of the sky by savage German fighter attacks and deadly antiaircraft fire. In short, the skies over Europe were a killing field, and it was the highest priority of the AAF to give this new fodder the minimum amount of training needed before they were rushed over to fill those vacant slots.

But unlike the individuals in single-seat fighters that were waging war in European skies, for those flying combat missions in the B-17, it was an enterprise carried out by a team of ten individuals who, at Alex, had to learn to subjugate their likes, dislikes, and prejudices while learning the skills needed to fly and defend their airplane. Their bomber had been named the Flying Fortress, a small airborne fort where those inside, armed with thirteen .50 caliber machine guns, were supposed to fight off the attacking hordes bent on destroying it. But this defense rests on the assumption that eight of the ten men, six of them with other jobs, can man those thirteen guns in a coordinated manner while under extreme stress at temperatures of fifty below zero, with deadly shrapnel exploding in the clouds around them and while being dived upon and shot at the German Luftwaffe aces. In the combat replacement crew training program, all of these ten individuals had to have one idea indelibly planted in their minds: the only way we have any chance of surviving what we are going into is for each crew member to *do his job or jobs, and do them to the absolute best of his ability*. In short, the need for survival has to be implanted while ten disparate individuals have to evolve into a tight social and functional team.

And every one of these teams has to have a leader with two skills. The first is to pilot the airplane, blindly a good percentage of the time, in tight formations, and through hellish conditions that would cause lesser men to collapse in fear or frustration. The second is the skill to coordinate the whole ten-man crew in such a way that it would always, even under the most adverse circumstances, function as a unit. These two skills, if the pilot has them, would not only compel the other nine men to respect him, but to follow his bidding blindly and without questions. Fortunately for Slats, the new crew had been assigned a pilot who would soon display those two skills to a very high degree.

His name was Francis N. Fridgen, still a second lieutenant, who was raised on a farm outside Dumont, Minnesota. He was "not tall," had a stocky build, was an estimated twenty-eight to thirty years old, unmarried, and a "very sharp" man who had studied engineering in college and "knew those Wright engines like a book." Soon they learned that he could handle their four-engine bomber with great skill. They also learned, after one or more of them started talking on the intercom,

*The New Crew*

that he was extremely strict about idle chatter. None of the crew was to say *anything* unless it was important for the mission's success.

The copilot was 2nd Lt. David E. Waller, also a "good" pilot, but "a bit cocky," and he "made no bones about his first choice, which was to be a fighter pilot." He was Slayton's height, with blondish hair, "likable personality," probably twenty-two or twenty-three years old, unmarried, and a native of New York City.

The bombardier, 2nd Lt. Phillip Palmer, who rode in the nose of the airplane below and in front of the pilot and copilot, was a "very likable guy" and a "great big guy—the biggest man on our crew." He, too, was twenty-two or twenty-three, unmarried, and from the Seattle area. He was also the worst shot on the skeet range, where at Fridgen's constant urging, the entire crew would spend many, many hours. And he was the one who was to aim and fire the two guns in the new chin turret that was now attached below the nose of all new-production B-17s. His main "tool" was the top-secret Norden bombsight, and if the airplane had to land in enemy territory, it was his duty to destroy it.

The navigator, 2nd Lt. Paul J. Ehmann (pronounced E-man), who also rode in the nose, was a "highly intelligent" man with an interesting background. At the estimated age of twenty-eight or twenty-nine he had already been in the army for several years, but in the U.S. Cavalry—which in the 1930s still rode horses. There, he had risen to the rank of captain, a rank from which "he took a bust" in order to transfer to the AAF. He was tall—"six or six-one and slender," and "very, very GI" who "believed in going by the book in everything"—a trait that was to dramatically change later. He was also married, with a pregnant wife in northern Florida, to where he longed to return.

The six enlisted crewmen all rode behind the four officers in the B-17.

Immediately behind the pilots was the flight engineer, Sgt. Robert Brennan, whose dual function was to monitor the engine and system instruments during takeoffs and landings, and while over enemy territory the electrical-powered top gun turret that had twin .50s. He was also to troubleshoot any mechanical or system problems that might arise during a mission. Slats grew to like Brennan, whom he called "a nice guy with a good personality." His home, like that of Waller, was New York City, and like Palmer, he was "real tall." Also, he was unmarried, as were all the enlisted men except the radio operator.

S.Sgt. William J. Reilly served as the radio operator: he manned the main radio and, also, the secret radio with which he used a telegraph key and which was to be destroyed if he ever had to abandon the airplane. When not at the radio, Sergeant Reilly had a secondary job, manning a single .50 from a mount in the top of the fuselage. Reilly was older than the other enlisted men, a red-headed Irishman from Canada. "He was a real robust, very cocky person and thought he could whip anybody—a typical Irish roughneck that swore a lot. He couldn't get his citizenship papers when first in service because he had been caught smuggling liquor into the U.S. after prohibition, but just before we went overseas, we were all given eight-day furloughs. He used that time to go to New Orleans where, somehow, he got his citizenship papers. After that he said, 'If I'm going to be a part of this damn crew, I had to be a citizen.' Of course I didn't know my butt from third base, but he was not my type—put it that way."

S.Sgt. Garrett M. Bartle was the ball turret gunner, and Slats could not remember if he was from one of the Carolinas or Virginia. "He and I were more alike than any of the others;

we were quieter and he loved the ball turret like I loved the tail position. If I had a real buddy on that crew, Bartle was it. And I think everybody on the crew liked him."

S.Sgt. Walter H. Abernathy, the right waist gunner, was born and raised in Tupelo, Mississippi. "He was about my age, but taller than me and blond, and he was also close to Bartle, whose station was just below him. The only problem he had was his deep Southern accent. He was teased about it a lot and seemed to handle it well, but in a private talk with me, he thought the rest of the crew overdid it, especially when one—he did not give a name—called it a n—— accent."

Finally, there was S.Sgt. Oliver Gaby, the left waist gunner and "the only one of the crew that I had a problem with," Slats admitted. Gaby was from Fort Wayne, Indiana, was about Slats's height and age, and had also gone to armament school. After Fridgen looked at all the crew members' school records before making assignments, he not only put Slats in the tail, which was considered the most vulnerable part of the airplane in a fighter attack (this changed as German fighter tactics evolved), but he also made Slats the first armorer, whose job was to supervise maintenance of all the guns and, when the plane was airborne on the way to a mission, to unscrew the pins that would allow the bomb propellers to turn when they were released. Gaby constantly reminded Slats that he, too, was qualified to do this job and implied that he could do it better. Slats ignored him for the most part, but one day they almost got into a fistfight before Reilly stepped in to separate them. "I felt a bit sorry for him sometimes," Slats said. "He was a loner most of the time and should have been on a different crew."

Slats himself was also a bit of a loner, and whereas some of the crewmen might have felt isolated and lonely in the cramped tail gunner's cabin, accessible only by crawling through the narrow area beside the retractable tail wheel, Slats liked being back there by himself. In a gunner's position, sitting on an oversize bicycle seat with his knees on pads built into the floor, and while holding the handles of his two guns with his arms wrapped around the rectangular, one-inch-thick tempered steel armor plate, he enjoyed having his private little refuge all to himself. He had been both happy and proud when Fridgen picked him to protect the most vulnerable part of the airplane. And, yes, this responsibility weighed on him, but he was no longer the five-foot-two freckle-faced boy with red peach fuzz on his cheeks. In the past eight months he had literally grown out of his boyhood. He still had the freckles, but his manly size, combined with the exceptional scores he had earned in all the mental and physical challenges in his training, had washed away much of the inferiority complex that hounded his past. He was a man now, and while standing around joking and bantering with the other nine members of his crew, he was buoyed by his new feelings of self-confidence. With the male hormones of post-puberty now energizing his systems, he felt fully ready to take on whatever challenges were lying in his future.

And his first challenge was to step up in front of the eight men manning guns in the airplane and explain how he wanted them to care for their weapons. In a new voice brimming with confidence, he told them exactly how they were to take their guns to the storage hut and oil them. They were told to apply the oil generously, but then, when they went to retrieve them for the next mission, they were to wipe them until all the parts looked dry. "They'll still have a thin coating of oil—enough to make them shoot properly but not enough to get thick and sticky in the cold air." Growing up in Fargo he knew firsthand what happens to oil in temperatures below forty, and

*The New Crew*

he probably added some relevant comments about that to add emphasis to his lesson. "I never had any trouble when I gave those orders to Palmer or Ehmann, the two officers who had to take care of guns, but later, since Ehmann, as navigator, was always the last one out of the briefings, I decided to take over the maintenance of his guns—which he really appreciated.

The crew had eight weeks at Alex to practice their teamwork. Most days they flew practice bombing missions to various destinations and targets that were briefed. And nearing the target, sighting in his technologically advanced Norden bombsight, Palmer first opened the bomb bay doors and then, with the target centered, he pretended to salvo a load of bombs. Slats cannot remember any towed banners being fired at for practice, but he does remember a number of missions over the Gulf where they could fire their guns without worrying about potential injury to civilians from falling bullets. He thinks that they mostly fired at oil slicks but admits that there could have been other targets.

The flying was refreshing because at altitude the air was cool. But, with no air conditioning anywhere on the field, and with both the temperature and the humidity at or near a hundred degrees, their ground time was just plain miserable. "Our clothes were always damp with sweat and there was no way to escape it. Then, if we had to get in the plane anytime near midday, it was like a sauna." But in the off-duty hours, they found a reprieve. There were two places downtown that had air conditioning, the Bentley Hotel and the Club Almanac. According to Slats's memory, both places were making a mint hosting the big partiers from the new air base.

Slats also remembers two breaks in the monotony of the long, boring training missions. On one occasion the sirens sounded and all crews reported to their airplanes to discover that a hurricane was forecast to be on its way and that they were to evacuate the base. His crew and maybe all the others—he is not sure—were ordered to fly a mission and land at Midwest Air Depot (now the Tinker Air Force Base) just outside Oklahoma City. However, after landing, they were trucked to quarters, and then dispersed to the officer and NCO clubs, the base commander, seeing all the Alex men out of dress uniform—they were wearing their flying clothes—ordered the Military Police to arrest them. Fortunately the Alex base commander was there and "raised holy hell," and the order was rescinded. Slats thinks they stayed there two nights, went to a downtown movie one of those nights, and left on the third day. When they returned to Alex, the wind was still raging and Fridgen demonstrated to his crew his exceptional piloting skills when he made a perfect landing.

Their second break came when they flew a long mission to Morris Field Air Base outside Charlotte, North Carolina. After landing, someone discovered that the Coca-Cola Band of the Week was playing at an outdoor dance pavilion in Charlotte. "Can we go, sir? Can we go?" Fridgen must have heard those pleas before he decided that the men deserved a break—and he could justify letting them attend by rationalizing that they also needed night flying experience. So, they all loaded up and somehow got to the dance where Shep Fields and His Rippling Rhythm band were playing. Girls were everywhere and everybody but Slats immediately went after them. Then, while he was standing on the sidelines just listening to the band, a "good-looking girl" grabbed him by the arm and pulled him out to the dance floor. He pleaded that he did not know how to dance and that he had never danced, but she did not give up. And when the song ended and he walked her back to the sidelines, she told him that he had good rhythm. "I probably smiled inside when she told me that," he admitted, "but I never danced again."

They flew home after the dance, landing back in the heat and humidity, and they got in several hours of credit for their night flying.

Eventually their crew training came to an end and they were given eight-day furloughs that Slats used to visit his mother in Fargo. But one more incident stands out clearly in his mind. When he got on the crowded train out of Alex and finally found a seat, a woman soon came down the aisle and stopped beside him. It was obvious that she could not find a seat and would have to stand in the aisle, at least to their next stop. Without even thinking about it, Slats stood up and invited the woman to take his seat. He recalls that she probably looked a bit frightened but he thought nothing of it until he looked around at the other passengers. "They were staring daggers at me," he said. "You can't believe the mean and angry looks I got all the way to the next stop." Then he realized what was going on. The woman he gave his seat to was a black woman. And this was Louisiana, where "n—— were taught to keep their place." He had grown up in a city where there was one black man who was genuinely liked by everybody. He had had no idea that he was committing an unforgivable social sin in Louisiana when he got up and offered that black woman his seat.

## CHAPTER 5

## Off to Ridgewell

When Fridgen's crew—they would not become Fridgen's Pigeons until later—returned to Alex from their furloughs, they were expecting to be given a new B-17 from the factory, spend a few days breaking it in, then fly the northern route through Maine, Labrador, and Iceland (or Greenland) to Ireland, then on to whatever Royal Air Force base they were to be assigned. Looking back, Slats thinks the whole crew was excited about that impending flight. It would be an adventure, and they would see parts of the world that they would never have otherwise seen.

So they waited. And they waited. Slats thinks it was ten days or more just doing nothing but lying around. And then they were called together on the flight line and Fridgen had an announcement. They were not going to get a new airplane. They were not going to get any kind of an airplane. They were going to take a troop train to New York City and they were going cross the Atlantic on a troopship.

We will never know the exact language that was expelled from the disappointed crew. Slats remembers that it "wasn't pretty." When asked to grade the level of disappointment he just said that he, personally, was greatly disappointed and believes the rest of the crew felt the same way. After all, they would now have to endure a several-days-long train trip, then a slow, boring voyage "packed like sardines" down in the hold of a ship—somehow they had heard horror stories about the miseries involved—and there was also the well-known danger of German U-boats, a danger that they did not know had greatly diminished when aerial reconnaissance planes got equipped with sub-finding radar in late 1942 and early 1943.

But orders were orders, so they packed their barracks bags, and with an estimated half-dozen crews—sixty men—they boarded a troop train in Alex and spent two or three days traveling to New York. However, this time they were treated to a luxury probably none had experienced; they had berths to sleep in during their nighttime travel. And when they finally got to the loading dock in New York City, walking with their barracks bags on their shoulders, they found lines and lines of ground troops and AAF personnel waiting to board what they believed to be the largest ship in the world: the *Queen Mary*.

The *Queen Mary* and the *Queen Elizabeth* had been the two flagships of the famous Cunard Line that transported tourists and vacationers all over the world, but mainly between London and New York. After U.S. military logistics planners saw the huge need to transport hundreds of thousands of military personnel to Europe, they arranged for the Cunard folks to take the *Queen Mary* to Australia, where it was gutted of its furniture, fine china, and other tourist accoutrements, painted a gray color like navy ships, and belted with a degaussing strip that demagnetized it so it would not attract dangerous magnetic mines that were being laid by the Germans. At the time it was officially the fastest ship in the world and it routinely hauled fifteen to sixteen thousand men from

New York City to Gourock, Scotland, which was about twenty-eight miles west of Glasgow.

After they embarked, Slats and the other enlisted crewmen were to find hammocks in what had been a lounge somewhere in the bowels of the ship, and began a zigzag cruise across the Atlantic that, according to the ship's log that has been preserved, took five days, seven hours, and thirty-six minutes to go 3,408 miles at an average speed of 26.7 knots. Slats and his crew were told the reasoning for the zigzag course: a German U-boat needed seven minutes to "draw a bead" on a ship with the *Queen Mary*'s speed, so to keep that from happening, the captain changed course every seven minutes.

Conditions during the journey were basically "terrible." Two meals a day were served, but for each, the men had to stand in line "at least for an hour but probably longer." Slats clearly remembers only standing in line for the morning meal, then supplementing it with apples, oranges, bananas, or candy bars that could be purchased at various locations around the ship. And, like all the others buried in the bowels, he was allowed one trip to the top deck to see one of the wonders of the world. "When I got up there, I was taken to where I could see the ship's wake. It was awesome: it went on for miles, and it was huge. Before or since I have never seen anything like it." Asked to describe what else he saw, he said, "Ground troops were living on the top deck, some playing craps, and I was glad I wasn't one of them."

During the trip he remembers passing his twentieth birthday, which was on October 30. But, only he knew it; he says that he never would have "made a fuss" about it with his fellow crew members.

The log says that they docked in Gourock, Scotland on November 2, but for the replacement aircrews buried with the thousands of other men in the ship's bowels, reaching

*Off to Ridgewell*

Scotland was an anticlimax. "It took days and days, maybe a week, before all of those guys could get off the ship and get transportation to wherever they were going. Then when we finally did get off, there was a miserably cold wind blowing, and the chill was made worse by the dampness. And as we waited for transportation to Glasgow where we were to board a train to Edinburgh and then London, they gave us K rations." None of the AAF men had ever seen these three-meals-in-a-box-type food rations before, and as they rode in trucks to the train station in Glasgow, and later, as trains took them to Edinburgh and London, they probably icked and yucked and made bad jokes about some of the ingredients such as the fatty pork loaf and the acidy lemon powder that most GIs at the time detested. And Slats was to discover a new type of money that he would later use to great advantage. Each meal packet had a four-pack of cigarettes. Slats did not smoke at the time, and most men who did smoke often burned up a normal twenty-cigarette pack every day. With the K rations holding just twelve cigarettes, the addicted smokers went into trading mode, and on that two- or three-day trip, Slats thinks he was able to enjoy the pleasure of some extra chocolate bars for dessert.

And how did Scotland look to him? "I knew I was in a foreign land. Everything seemed so old. The buildings looked like they had been built three or four centuries earlier. And the golf courses—the heather was so tall I said to myself, 'Hell's fire, who is going to try and hit a ball out of that crap?' And the speech. The crews were real nice to us, but they talked fast, not slow like we did, and it was a totally different jargon. Like, going to the bathroom—we had to learn to ask for the loo. And the trains looked funny. The seats were made of heavy wood and it was like sitting in a church pew. I sure knew I was no longer in Fargo, North Dakota—I was thinking I'd rather live in Fargo at fifty below than in this kind of country. Even the people looked like foreigners. They were dressed with big sweaters, knickers, big heavy socks, and everybody wore a hat or cap. I really felt like I was in a foreign land and I began to think that I wasn't going to like it. Some of the guys even joked that we should cut down all of the barrage balloons that floated over the cities and let the island sink."

Slats thinks they traveled all night getting to London but cannot remember anything about the transfer to the train that took them to Cambridge. He does remember the twenty-eight-mile truck ride to his new base southeast of Cambridge. Its name was Ridgewell, which was the town a few miles west of it, but it was closer to the village of Great Yeldham that had a pub, the Wagon and Horses Hotel, that Slats and his crew would soon discover.

He and the other members of his crew were shocked when they first saw their new base. "The first things we saw were the Nissen huts, then when we got closer I was amazed that it was so spread out, I mean it looked like all the planes were parked a hundred yards from each other. We found out later that this was a defensive arrangement against German bombs—a bomb could get one plane, but that's about all."

Soon they were gathered at base supply, picking up another barracks bag and a duffel bag full of their flight gear—wool long johns, fleece-lined pants, jackets, boots, gloves, caps, and an electrically heated flight suit. "Boy, after carrying all that stuff around for a while, we really were worn out," Slats said, remembering that long afternoon. Also, he and his crew got an awakening. In line with them were well over a hundred men, all replacement crews. But then they discovered that seventy of the men, including themselves, were replacement crews for the 533rd Squadron. This was just one of the four squadrons in their 381st Bomb Group, which occupied the

Ridgewell base. But seventy men—seven new crews? They probably never asked anybody: Why so many new crews? They had to know the reason: they had to know that these seven new crews were now going to fill the shoes of seventy other men whose bombers had been shot out of the sky. Clearly the reality of their impending fate was upon them.

And what was that reality? They had just joined one of the thirty-nine bomb groups in the Eighth Air Force, all of which were based in this same region of England. And what was the Eighth's mission? From their earliest days in England, eleven weeks after Pearl Harbor, their goal was to conduct strategic bombing raids over Germany and German-occupied territory. And what did the term "strategic" mean? It meant that the goal of the Eighth was to destroy targets that were so important to the German war effort that the destructive effects would be multiplied several times.

Example: the German oil industry. If the plants that were refining crude oil, for instance the oil from wells in German-occupied Romania, as well as the plants that were producing synthetic oil from Germany's vast coal supplies, were totally destroyed by bombing, what would happen to the mobility of the whole German army? No tanks could run, no trucks would be carrying supplies, and no fighter planes could defend the country. In other words, if the oil industry were destroyed by bombing, the German army would be totally paralyzed.

Another example of a strategic target was critical parts of the machinery of war. Like ball bearings. Every moving wheel, whether as small parts of a big machine or the main wheels of vehicles, had to have ball bearings. And if the ball bearing factories were all destroyed? No new equipment for the army.

A third example was the aircraft industry producing the Messerschmitts, Focke-Wulfs, and other Luftwaffe fighters. When Slats arrived at Ridgewell, the cross-channel invasion of

France was scheduled for the coming May, roughly six months later. But what would happen during this invasion if the Luftwaffe ruled the skies over them? Allied planners knew that the invasion could fail, even without the Luftwaffe overhead, so they did not want to even consider a cross-channel invasion unless the Luftwaffe could be taken out of the equation. To support the coming invasion, the bombing and destruction of the airplane factories was a critical strategic necessity.

Then there were the railroad marshaling yards—big areas where trains could assemble, switch tracks, and be routed to various destinations. After the cross-channel invasion, the Germans would send a horde of trains carrying reinforcements of tanks, artillery, and men to the battle sites—unless the marshaling yards were destroyed. Until they would be repaired, reinforcements would be slowed, if not stalled, thus protecting the heavier side of the invasion equation.

However, all aspects of the strategic bombing concept were just that: concepts. The reality—the strategy that was being used to carry out the strategic concept—was almost disastrous because of two basic miscalculations on the part of those who implemented the plan. First, from the time the four-engine B-17 came to England to bomb the strategic targets, leaders of the AAF like the Chief of Staff Gen. Henry H. "Hap" Arnold and the general leading the Eighth Air Force, Ira C. Eaker, successfully argued against British leaders, including Prime Minister Winston Churchill, that the "Fort," because of all its guns, could defend itself from Luftwaffe fighter attacks and could get to the targets and back without fighter escort. The British counterargument was that until a long-range fighter was developed that could escort the bombers to and from their targets deep in Germany, the Eighth should copy what the Brits were doing: they should bomb at night when, with the exception of a few night fighters the Germans had developed, they would be free of the fighter onslaught. However, at a Casablanca summit in January 1943, where the generals met with President Roosevelt and Churchill, General Eaker, in a memo to Churchill, used the phrase "around the clock bombing" in his argument that Churchill should change his mind and support the Eighth's strategy of daylight bombing. Historians now think that phrase lit lights in Churchill's mind and caused him to back off on his argument with Roosevelt to change the Eighth's strategy. From that day forward, for better or worse—mostly worse—the around-the-clock bombing by the Brits at night and the Americans by day would continue and never be seriously challenged again.

The strategy had another flaw. By all accounts the Norden bombsight was an engineering marvel, and when properly used, could cause bombs to fall on or very close to any kind of stationary target. But there was one very important caveat: *the bombardier had to be able to see the target*. And what Eighth Air Force planners tended to ignore was the fact that strategic bombing targets in and around Germany were covered by clouds much of the time, especially in the colder six months of the year. And yes, there were some helpful technological developments, including a primitive radar system that would allow a bombardier to differentiate between the water and shoreline of port cities. But despite glowing reports from the Eighth's public relations folks, the bitter truth was that much of the time the American bombardiers were not sighting targets on their Nordens, but, instead, were dropping when a lead bombardier salvoed his bombs. So, basically, because of the spread-out formations, this was area bombing, not precision bombing.

Consideration of all this, of course, was way above the pay grades of the Fridgen crew. And they had better things to do than worry about the combat that they would soon be entering. Flying a bomber from a base covered in clouds most of the time, and then joining up with two hundred or three hundred or four hundred other bombers in formation, required lessons and practice that had not been included in the Alex curriculum. Slats and the other gunners were essentially going to be tourists, riding in the back of their bomber, and looking down on the normally beautiful bright and white November undercast, while their pilots and navigator were mastering their lessons on formation flying.

## CHAPTER 6

## Into the Deadly Skies

It would be twenty-four days before Slats was to see his first combat. During that time, he and his crew flew many practice missions, with Fridgen and Waller as pilots and Ehmann as navigator learning how to meet and rendezvous with the other new crews in the 381st. But what Slats remembers the most about those days is the hours and hours they spent on the skeet range. Using 12-gauge Model 12 Winchester pump guns, they shot hundreds and hundreds of shells at the clay pigeons from every conceivable angle. Why all this shooting? It was their leader who was so passionate about these efforts. Slats speculates that most of his motivation was legitimate, that leading and shooting at high-speed moving targets would help those who would be doing the same thing in defense of their airplane. "But Fridgen was a farm boy who had grown up in Minnesota wing-shooting pheasants and quail, and so he was a damn good shot. I could never beat him even though I way outshot the others on the crew. I think his love of shooting had to be a part of the reason why we spent so much time out there. We enjoyed it, too—except maybe for Palmer (the tall bombardier), who never would get the gunstock solidly against his arm and ended up with painful bruises. I used to laugh when he'd say to me, 'Slayton, how can you shoot so much and not be hurting like I am?' I tried to explain what he was doing wrong but don't think it had any effect."

Besides the flying and the skeet shooting there were the mundane routines that had to be performed. In their Nissen hut six enlisted members of one crew slept on single beds on one side, while another crew's six members shared the other side. In the middle at one end was a small coal stove, and they had a weekly ration of coke "that was good for about one night." Fortunately, there was a "fella in the other crew who was an expert at pilfering coke—I can't think of his name. Anyway, we'd ask him where he got it and he'd say, 'I'm not gonna tell you guys, I have to do it on the QT.' So, because of him, we were able to stay fairly warm most nights—but we still laid on our beds reading or whatever with our clothes on because you had to be close to the stove to really get warm. That damp air in wintertime England was damn miserable."

Also during this pre-mission period crew dynamics came into play. Slats is adamant that the bonds between the crew grew much stronger than at Alex. They did everything together, they sat together at meals, they kept together on the flight line, and they soon started walking the mile or so to the pub in Great Yeldham, or "Yoho." At this same time they also experienced some negative crew dynamics: "First off, when we got there, we felt like strangers because the regular crews already there didn't seem like they wanted to accept us. I thought they should have liked us more than they did and it bothered us. But it also helped strengthen the bonds between us. Basically, we thought the hell with them; if they don't like us, tough—we've got each other."

Slats did become good friends with one of the other crew members who shared their hut. "His name was Jack Trueblood and he was from South Dakota. He was also a tail gunner, so besides the part of the country we came from, we had that in common." Unfortunately, his new friend was destined to be blown out of the sky by a flak burst.

Their first mission was on December 11 to Emden, Germany, where they would try to destroy moored submarines along with the supporting facilities. Flying in the tail, one piece of his flak suit under his seat and the other two draped on two sides of him, Slats had no idea what to expect. Then, in the process of forming up, another airplane suddenly came in behind them and he quickly told Fridgen, "'Get the tail up because we've got a guy back here about to smash into me.' He said, 'Roger,' then he came up with the tail and the other guy dropped down." And that was about all the excitement they experienced on the whole mission. Unbeknown to the enlisted crew, they were being led to the target by one or two Pathfinder bombers—bombers equipped with the new H2S radar. Because Emden was on a sheltered cove of the North Sea the radar could identify the target through the undercast. However, as it turned out, "there wasn't a cloud in sight and we demolished those submarine pens. And yes, we saw a little flak, but not a single enemy fighter. We didn't lose a single plane, and what a milk run! I'm sure we were all thinking, 'Boy, if we could do twenty-five of those, wouldn't it be great.'" What Slats did not know was that they did not see enemy fighters because of the swarm of P-47 Thunderbolts in addition to some of the new long-range P-51 Mustangs that were escorting them. Apparently, the Luftwaffe had no desire to tangle with this mass of American fighters.

In sum, their first entrance into the deadly skies was a gentle one.

And they also lucked out on the second and third missions to the submarine assembly yards in Bremen—intelligence from secret radio intercepts had informed the Allies that the Germans were now building submarines with new technology allowing them to remain submerged for up to seventy-two hours, which would prevent them from being detected by airborne radar. These were potentially very dangerous new weapons and destroying them became a very high priority. Slats and airplanes from his squadron flew to Bremen on December 13 and then again three days later. They were again led by Pathfinders, and both times they bombed through a solid overcast. "Actually," Slats remembers, "I never ever saw a target on any mission after that first one to Emden." Both these missions were "gentle"; they saw some flak but did not encounter enemy fighters.

But after the first mission to Bremen, Slats was so tired, that after the debriefing—and no, he never got the shot of booze that later crews would enjoy afterward—he dragged himself to his hut and went to bed, still hearing his crewmen's words ringing in his ears: "You're missing your fried chicken, you're missing your fried chicken." Now, he says, "I loved the fried chicken we got after every mission, but the stress of those missions—just the anticipation of attacks and the anxiety or fear that I might miss seeing an attacking fighter—that's what wore me out. I was just pooped after every mission. Sometimes, when I did eat, I was so tired I could hardly lift a piece of chicken. It's just hard to explain what that anxiety can do to you."

Fridgen's crew flew their fourth mission on December 24, the day before Christmas. It was a short mission over to Cocove, France, against some rocket gun installations, and while they encountered a lot of flak, they never saw any enemy fighters. The 533rd squadron did have to go over the

54

*Into the Deadly Skies*

target three times before they could release their bombs, an act that caused their bombardier, Palmer, to mutter over the intercom, "I'm getting tired of this." But they escaped damage from the flak and returned home to enjoy a special Christmas eve dinner of ham, which Slats managed to enjoy since, because of the shortness of the mission, his body did not feel drained.

Their fifth mission, on December 30, was to Ludwigshafen to bomb a chemical complex; with 710 airplanes in the attacking formation, it was possibly the largest group of bombers yet assembled. Said Slats, "We were in the high group and I was tail-end Charlie—I mean at the very back end. I could look down out my windows and I never saw so damned many airplanes in all my life." Their route took them across the corner of France, then out into the Atlantic before they turned toward the target, a diversionary measure designed to confuse the opposition. And there was opposition after they got closer to the target. "I was looking up," said Slats, "and could see this contrail, then pretty soon I saw another contrail behind the first one. As I watched, the first airplane must have seen the guy behind him because he immediately dived down toward our formation, the other guy right behind him. I mean, they were moving and I soon got worried because the German plane, an FW-190, was coming right at us, a P-47 right on his tail—there was no way any plane could outdive a P-47. They both went right by my tail and just as I looked down to the right, the P-47 was so close it looked like he was going to ram the guy. Then he fired and the P-47 just blew him to pieces—what a beautiful sight to watch—I never enjoyed watching anything so much."

As they continued on, the flak got heavier and after they made their bomb run and turned back to the west, flak bursts were still all around them. "I didn't know if any of it hit us,"

Slats said. "Back in the tail it was so noisy that I couldn't have heard it like the guys up front." Luckily, they escaped getting damaged, but all the way home they bucked a strong headwind and were low on fuel when they finally landed. "It seemed like it must have been an eight- or ten-hour mission [according to another group's log it was probably closer to seven and a half hours] because I was so tired I could hardly stand up when I got out—but I had been on my knees all that time." What Slats never knew was that despite all those airplanes dropping bombs, the chemical complex at Ludwigshafen was not touched and twenty-three bombers were lost.

After the truck dumped them off at their quarters, Slats probably collapsed on his bed and failed again to enjoy the after-mission fried chicken. But the next day they lucked out and were not one of the seven crews from their squadron called to fly on the "very long" mission to strike an airfield outside Bordeaux, France. So, to celebrate the completion of their "air medal mission"—air medals were automatically awarded after completion of five missions—they celebrated New Year's Eve by walking to the pub in Yoho. There, after persistent teasing by his crew, Slats finally decided to try one of the ales that the others were drinking. "The first one tasted pretty good so I had a second and a third, and although they said that I became a lot more talkative, I can remember saying, 'This stuff doesn't do anything to excite me.' So I have another one or two and then it hit me like a ton of bricks. When we stagger back to the base, I'm bombed out but I somehow made it to my sack. The next morning, I'm hung over, but I became a regular beer drinker after that."

The 533rd Squadron *War Diary* describes New Year's Day in the squadron: "Many men of the squadron awoke to greet 1944 with furry tongues and throbbing noggins, after sessions in the pubs of Cambridge, Ridgewell, and 'Yoho,' as

Great Yeldham is called. Those whose stomachs weren't repelled by the sight of food enjoyed hot cakes, with butter and syrup, for breakfast and a full-course turkey dinner at noon . . . some twenty-seven enlisted men of the 533rd left on eight-day furloughs."

Slats remembers the turkey dinner but doubts that he felt well enough to get up the next morning for the pancakes. He also remembers a very moving experience that happened sometime after the New Year. "I was in the combat crew lounge and picked up a pamphlet that was titled *ARC London Light*. This was a news pamphlet from the American Red Cross, and as I started reading it, I saw this article about the Hans Crescent Golf Team defeating some university team and Frank Cormaci of the 381st Bomb Group shot a 69 and Don Slayton of the 109th Reconnaissance Squadron shot a 70. That really got my attention. I knew Don was in England—my mother wrote me, but the censors blacked out his address and my address—I guess they thought that should be top-secret information. Anyhow, this guy Cormaci is on my base, so I go to the bartender and ask him if he could tell me how I might find this guy and he says, 'Hell yes, he's a debriefer and he's a bunk buddy of mine. Here, let me draw you a map.' So he draws this map, I get on my bicycle and ride down to this Nissen hut, go in, and this guy lying on a bunk looks at me and says, "Well, I'll be damned, I've just met the redhead's brother." That just floored me, but Don and I did look a bit alike, especially with both of us having red hair and freckles. So we visit for a while and he says he'll be seeing Don the coming Sunday when they play another match and he would tell Don how to find me. I was pretty excited because, even though he was quite a bit older, I felt almost as close to him as I did to Einer, and I hadn't seen him for almost eight years—since he left and took the golf pro job in

Lewistown, Montana. Then, the next Monday—we weren't flying a mission and when I was lying on my bunk reading, somebody tapped me on the shoulder. I turned and it was Don. We were really happy to see each other and we sat and chatted for a long time. Then I asked how often he played golf. He said that they played every Sunday—usually college teams—and he said he had even gone up to Scotland and played the famous St. Andrews course. Then I made him an offer. I said that the next time I got a forty-eight [forty-eight-hour pass] for the weekend I'd come to London and caddy for him. He agreed, then I told him that I would be staying at the Hans Crescent Club—a USO Club in London—I had been there on a forty-eight before we started flying missions and really liked the place. So we did that."

Slats then went on to tell what happened when he caddied for Don the first time.

"He was playing two students from Cambridge University, their best ball against his best ball. So we get to this par five and he hits a drive, it seems like it went almost 300 yards, and when we got to the ball I handed him a four-iron. The other guys laugh, saying that they had never seen anybody get on the green in two on this par five. So Don hits that four-iron and puts it 20 feet from the pin, and these two guys go crazy. But Don had big arms and wrists, and while he was a pro in Lewistown, he had won a long-drive competition with three drives 298-299-305—and remember, this was with the clubs and ball as they were back then. Don beat them badly—I don't remember the scores—and when we got in, the president of the club had me sign the guest book with Don because he had never before had two brothers from America at his club."

## CHAPTER 7

## Brutal Skies

Slats was a sound sleeper, but there was a special noise, not overly loud, that always brought him out of a deep sleep. It was the sound of the electric generators that came on about three or four o'clock in the morning before a mission was to be flown. Then, while awake and listening to the rumble, rumble, rumble, the painful waiting began. Would it be their hut the Charge of Quarters (CQ) was going to enter and, "with some smart-ass comment, announce, 'Okay, Fridgen's Pigeons (the crew was now being called by that name), drop your cocks and grab your socks, you're gonna be flying today.'"

When those generators started the morning of January 4, they might also have heard rain tinkling on their metal roof—rain was almost an everyday occurrence in England at that time of the year. Then the sound they most dreaded came. The CQ, the most hated man in the squadron, opened their door, and while Slats cannot remember his special refrain that day, he is certain that it was obnoxious enough that the crew would have wanted to throw a boot at him.

Then it was dress and hike to the mess hall where a pre-mission breakfast of fried eggs with bacon or ham would usually be one of the two treats they got on mission days. Of course, it would be pitch black after that when the truck would take the gunners to their airplane—Reilly, the radio operator, would go to a special briefing as would the four officers. The gunners would go to the gun shack, carefully wipe off all the excess oil, then mount the guns in their airplane. As he had done back in Alex, Slats would always do Lieutenant Ehmann's guns first, then mount his twin .50s in the tail.

The rest of the crew came and the preflight routine began. As usual Slats had placed his flak jacket pieces where he thought they would best protect him, his parachute on a shelf on the left front side, and his brogans in the narrow area behind him. Next, the engines started and it was then "taxi a few feet, brake squeak, brake squeak, taxi a few feet, brake squeak, brake squeak . . ." But then there was a noise that those up front could hear, and Fridgen came over the intercom saying, "I think something happened up front." And something did happen, something terrible. A bomber from another squadron, the crew on their twenty-fifth and last mission, was taking off, an engine caught fire, they sal-voed their bombs, and then, because with three engines they were still overloaded with all their fuel, they couldn't gain altitude and caught some trees that sent them down, caus-ing a violent explosion. All this they found out later, but this tragedy caused the commanders to begin requiring all those behind the bomb bay to sit on the floor of the radio room during takeoff in order to improve climbing performance.

Airborne, Slats learned that they were heading to another German port city, Kiel, where the H2S radar in the Pathfinders could identify their submarine target at the waterline—Kiel was at the end of a deep fjord near the Danish border. En route, they did not encounter any enemy fighters, but the flak was "horrible." Somehow they made it through the clouds of flak over the target, but then their luck ran out. As they were pulling away a blast hit them, immediately damaging engines two and three—the two inboards—that had to be feathered. Slats remembers what happened next like it had happened yesterday. After Fridgen feathered the two engines, Reilly came on the intercom and said, "Let's go to Sweden and sit out the war." Fridgen quickly came on the intercom and told Reilly to shut up, then, very calmly, asked Ehmann for a heading to the nearest English base and an ETA—estimated time of arrival. "I couldn't believe how fast Ehmann came back with the answer, giving him a heading and the ETA. That man was quick. He was ready with that information in seconds. He really knew what he was doing."

Then Fridgen came on the intercom with an announcement to the whole crew, saying something to the effect that "it's going to be a close one and water may be hitting the ball turret before we get there, but I think we can just make it." That announcement really caught Slats's attention, because if they had to ditch, the first one out was the tail gunner and "I wasn't a good swimmer. Yeah, I had to learn; I had to be able to swim one lap and back in order to graduate from high school, but the North Sea? I will admit it: I was scared."

They were flying by themselves now, and Fridgen had both good engines running at maximum manifold pressure and RPM, and sometime on the way back, he said that they would not be flying in this airplane soon, if ever, because he was going to burn out the two outboards in order to get them back to England. Sometime after that, they all looked out to their three o'clock position where a P-38 had stationed itself as their protector, and to report their position if they had to ditch. "I am pretty sure he feathered one engine just to stay with us," said Slats. "In fact, I'm almost positive that he did."

They got lower and lower as they approached England, but Ehmann had given them a course to an English air base and while dangerously low, Fridgen greased it in, breaking up a soccer game that the English crews were playing on the runway. Immediately, Fridgen came on the intercom, saying that he thought he hit and ruined their soccer ball—an announcement that brought laughs and broke the tension all of them had been feeling.

After they parked and exited the airplane, all the crew members but Slats began examining and counting the flak holes. Slats remembers that he did not join them, probably because he did not want to see the damage. Instead, he started bantering with a young Englishman who came up to him, announced that he was also a tail gunner, and that his .30 caliber guns could fire a helluva lot faster than Slats's slow .50s. "I came right back at him—I don't know if I called them pea-shooters or not, but I made it clear that my guns could do a helluva lot more damage than his .30s. Then I think he said that he had four .30s, but I may be way off base on that. Anyway, it was a friendly argument, and we were all treated well before trucks came and took us to Ridgewell, which could not have been much more than an hour or so away."

It would be ten days before they would fly again because the weather over Germany was so bad. Slats thinks that this was when his whole crew got a forty-eight and that the enlisted guys all went to London. Slats remembers partying with them one night at the Hans Crescent Club and that Brennan got drunk and went off with either one of the Red Cross girls or a girl who had come to dance with the men. Slats thinks he had "a beer or two," but his New Year's Eve experience caused him to be cautious. He also thinks that he caddied for Don again on his second day of leave.

Then, on the morning of January 11, the portable generators started rumbling and soon the CQ came to their hut. After one of his usual obscene refrains, he announced that Fridgen's Pigeons and McEvoy's crew were both flying this day. Lt. Matthew J. McEvoy was the pilot for the other six enlisted men in their hut, including tail gunner Jack Trueblood, whom Slats had gotten to know much better and whom he now considered his best friend in the squadron.

Slats went through the usual pre-mission routine in their new airplane that the crew had named Homing Pigeon, but out on the flight line the cold misty rain sent the gunners to one of the ground crew tents to try to stay dry—they did not want their clothes to freeze and get stiff when they got airborne.

After Reilly and the officers came and after they endured the agonizing taxi, brake-squeak sequence, they finally got airborne and the gunners took their positions. Fridgen then told them that they were going to Oschersleben, the main FW-190 assembly plant ninety miles west of Berlin, and that they were part of a seven-hundred-plane armada of B-17s and B-24s. He also told them they would have a fighter escort of P-47s and P-38s for much of the way, and that a single group of the new long-range P-51s would take them all the way to the target. Thinking back on that announcement, Slats said, "I think he was telling us that to make us feel good, but I knew, and I think the others realized, that the Germans would throw everything they had at us in order to protect that factory."

And that was literally what happened. Vicious fighter attacks first hit the armada over the Zuiderzee in Holland, and they continued sporadically during the next two and a half hours to their target. Slats remembers that he had a few chances to fire at those diving through their formation, but he also remembers that the nine airplanes in his squadron were tucked into such a tight formation that he had to hold back firing for fear that he would hit one of the two airplanes tucked in behind him. Then one of these airplanes, the one Slats knew was carrying McEvoy's crew, was attacked by a FW-190 and immediately caught fire and started spiraling down out of formation, the pilots probably killed or wounded. Slats watched in horror, for in that burning airplane, now engulfed in flames and from which he saw no parachutes emerge, was the hut's beloved coke snatcher, and Sgt. Jack G. Trueblood, Slat's best friend. "From then on," Slats said, "I think my mind was traumatized. I swear, the rest of that mission is just a blur, although I remember seeing others of our squadron also going down. It was just a bloodbath and, frankly, I have tried over the years to wipe it out of my mind."

The 533rd Squadron history says that six of the nine squadron airplanes were lost that day and because of the severity of the fire, they assumed that McEvoy's crew perished—killed in action (KIA), in military speak. A few days later, the 381st Group was awarded a Presidential Unit Citation, partly because they were credited for destroying twenty-eight German fighters on that mission. "We didn't think it was a big deal," Slats said. "They didn't pin anything on us; we were just told to go to the orderly room and get it. We all thought it was small potatoes considering there were sixty empty beds in our squadron."

It would be ten days before the squadron flew again, and with many new crews. In the Nissen hut where McEvoy's enlisted crew had been, a new crew led by 2nd Lt. Milton F. Tarr moved in to take the empty beds. And this is when Slats and his crew realized why they had been treated so coldly by the older crews when they first came to the squadron. "After seeing those guys going down," Slats said, "something happened to us. We didn't dislike these new guys; I think we were just hurting so much that we were afraid to develop any close relationships." But Slats does remember one member of the new crew with whom he did develop a relationship. "His name was Louis Benecke and he was from Dickinson, North Dakota. I took to him a bit."

Another thing happened after that mission to Oschersleben. Lieutenant Ehmann, who had been in the Regular Army cavalry before coming over to the USAF, up to this time had been more formal and more what his enlisted crew members described as little bit chicken-shit. But something changed in him after January 11. For one thing, he came to Slats and in a friendly, almost brotherly tone, said that he would like to come back in the tail early or late in some mission and see what it was like to ride back there. Slats, of course, welcomed the idea and said that he would crawl out and Ehmann could crawl in and try out his bicycle seat and kneepads. Then, sometime after that, when the men were going to the theater to see a movie, Ehmann asked if he could join them. They agreed even though they knew he was not supposed to sit with enlisted personnel. Ehmann sat down with them, but soon two military policemen (MPs), who must have been called by the manager, came down to where they were seated and told Ehmann politely that he could not stay there. Ehmann snapped back at them, saying something like, "If I fly and fight and run the risk of dying with these guys, I can sure as hell sit and watch a movie with them." But the MPs would not budge and said that the lieutenant was breaking regulations and that they would have to go back and report to his commander. Ehmann still sat there, defiant, then the ranking MP ordered him to stand up, but he would not do it. They ordered again, and when he finally rose, they both grabbed his arms and manhandled him out of the theater. Slats remembers that his strong desire to be with his enlisted crew greatly impressed them. And while they had a high respect for him as a navigator, especially after the Kiel raid when his guidance got them back without ditching, they now developed a special affection for him that they had not felt before.

Finally, on January 21, ten days after Oschersleben, Fridgen's Pigeons left Ridgewell on their eighth mission. They went after German targets on the French coast—part of the pre-invasion campaign that was on the Eighth's agenda. In the debriefing one squadron bombardier described it as a bombardier's dream—no cloud cover, meager flak, no enemy fighters, and repeated runs over the target that allowed pinpoint bombing. Slats only remembers the relief he felt because of the lack of fighters and flak, and the unusually long time they spent over the target. He thinks that he was able to enjoy the fried chicken after this mission.

The next day, January 22, he and three other gunners in his crew got news that sent them to the pub in Yoho for a celebration. Sergeants Gaby, Bartle, Abernathy, and Slayton got orders notifying them that they now had the rank of staff sergeant. And the celebration? Slats just remembers that he drank a lot of ale, and that he probably got just as "snockered" as he had been at the New Year's Eve party.

The records show that Fridgen's Pigeons flew to Frankfurt on January 29, then to Wilhelmshaven February 3, and back to Frankfurt again on February 4, the latter raid with more than a thousand bombers, but they are all a blur in Slats's memory. Yes, at Frankfurt both times, he remembers bombing through a heavy overcast and a sky so black with flak that he wonders how Homing Pigeon even made it through. And the raid to Wilhelmshaven has been completely erased from his mind. "I don't think I was what they called 'flak happy' at the time; I think I was mentally okay. But the tension and the losses . . . Lt. Robert P. Deering was one of two that went down on the second Frankfurt raid and I knew some of those guys—some nice fellows." Then, when he was reminded that their radioman was cited in the 533rd Squadron *War Diary* for bravery on the Wilhelmshaven mission, Slats remembered and describes the incident.

"I think I was mentally okay because I do remember something that happened to Sergeant Reilly, our radio man on that mission. We were carrying incendiaries, not high-explosive bombs, and when Lieutenant Palmer salvoed the bomb load over the target, four of the bombs got hung up in the bomb bay and he did not dare close the doors. Reilly, who was closest to the bomb bay and noticed the problem, took a walk-around oxygen bottle, climbed down into that forty-below-zero wind, and with one hand managed to pull each of them loose. He saved us but did not get a medal and he later reminded us several times of how put out he was that he wasn't honored for his bravery."

Four days after the second Frankfurt raid, on February 4, they were airborne again. Their twelfth mission was to a German airfield outside Nancy, France, more than two hundred miles east of Paris and almost at the German border. There, Slats remembers a heavy overcast and also knew from Fridgen's comments over the intercom that they had strict orders not to drop bombs blindly over a French target they could not see. After "several" flyovers, but with minimal flak and no fighters, they still could not jettison their load and carried them back to the Channel. After they landed, they were afraid that they would not be credited with a mission because they did not bomb the target, but they got what they considered a bonus: the Nancy mission was declared a combat mission.

They were soon to get another bonus—the whole crew was awarded an eight-day furlough. "I'm sure we all went to London, but we split up there. I did some touring, saw Buckingham Palace and 10 Downing Street, Churchill's headquarters. Also, one evening we went to the Carleton Theatre to see the Gary Cooper–Ingrid Bergman movie made of Hemingway's novel *For Whom the Bell Tolls*, and as we walked into the lobby there is General Eisenhower standing there—he was coming out. We all said, 'Hi, Ike,' and he just smiled and greeted us—with no offense that we called him that."

As usual, Slats stayed in a room at the Hans Crescent Club, but one evening he decided to visit the famous Rainbow Corner, a Red Cross club where a serviceman could find female companionship and a free meal any hour of the day. Like most of the visitors, he went to the ballroom to see the girls and the musicians and the dancers. And there, trying to be inconspicuous because he had no intention of trying to dance, a girl came up to him and tried to get him to the dance floor. However, unlike the girl who dragged him out a few months before, while they were in Charlotte, North Carolina, when Slats protested that he could not dance, this girl took him by the arm and they went off to a quiet corner where they could talk. And they talked and they talked—for two hours and maybe longer. "She was really a nice girl. Good-looking, too, with brown hair and brown eyes. I really think she grew to like me. When I got up to go—I wouldn't have had any idea how to take her home or anything—she wrote down her phone number and made me promise that I would call her the next time I came to London. That paper got lost and now I can't even remember her name."

Back in Ridgewell, in the early morning hours of February 22, the morbid sound of the electrical generators woke Slats and the rest of the enlisted crew. They all knew that the next mission would be their thirteenth, and so there was an extra dimension to their apprehension as they waited, dreading for the hated squadron CQ to come barging into their hut. They waited and they waited, and then he came. "Fridgen's Pigeons, *obscenity, obscenity,* you're flying today." One can only guess at the ugly rebuttal he received from the disappointed crew.

## CHAPTER 8

## The Final Mission

The reader has already flown part of mission 13 with Fridgen's Pigeons. On the way to Oschersleben and the FW-190 assembly plants, a rocket-launching, twin-engine Messerschmitt fired one of its ninety-pound rockets that went through the tail of Homing Pigeon, barely missing Slats and leaving a huge hole at his left front as it exited. The good news for the crew was that the timed fuse in the rocket did not trigger an explosion as the rocket went through the fuselage. The bad news was that, as it went through, it sliced the electrical, intercom, and oxygen connections to the tail section. No one could talk to Slats, his electrically heated suit no longer functioned in the fifty-below air blasting by his body, and he had passed out from anoxia and would soon die. When this situation was reported by waist gunner Abernathy, Fridgen immediately decided to risk the lives of the other nine by leaving the protection of the formation and diving to an altitude where Slats could breathe without supplementary oxygen. That is when the reader left the story in order to learn more about the man Fridgen was trying to save.

Slats began to regain consciousness in the screaming power dive. His mind was confused, he was disoriented, and for a moment he thought the airplane was out of control and diving toward the ground. Then his brain cells began to function again, and he felt the huge pressure as Fridgen began to pull out of the dive. "I thought I was going to go through the bottom of the tail," he said, recalling the experience and marveling at the strength of the wing and tail of the B-17 to withstand G force.

A minute or two after leveling off, the plane was attacked by twelve FW-190s, in a line on the left side of the airplane. They were firing as they came in, but Slats could not turn his guns far enough to the right to fire at them. He heard the others firing, and although he did not know it at the time, both Ehmann and Gaby were wounded by these first bursts. The third engine—the right inboard—was damaged and on fire. Afraid of an explosion, Fridgen gave the bail-out order. Brennan, Abernathy, and Reilly, who had superficial wounds, bailed out immediately. Bartle, coming out of his ball turret, went to Gaby, who had a severe abdominal wound, and tried to throw him out. But Gaby hung on tightly to the edge of the escape hatch and kept yelling for Bartle to go, which he finally did. This left the four officers in the nose, Gaby, and Slats. And then, just as he realized that his chute had been blown out by the rocket, but before he could even swing his guns around, one of the fighters dove in from the seven o'clock position and Slats felt pieces of one or more of the exploding shells hitting his right knee, his left thigh, and his right ring finger. He immediately looked down to examine the wounds while considering himself lucky that the armor must have absorbed most of the shrapnel that would otherwise have killed him. Then he squeezed his right hand, and blood spurted from his finger. While doing this, he had let go of his guns and they were hanging down. This, along with the gaping hole that must have been quite visible, probably convinced the pilot of another fighter that the tail gunner was dead and he could safely ease in close behind the bomber and finish it off. But Slats, though wounded, was angrier than he can ever remember being, and when that FW-190 got somewhere between a hundred and two hundred yards, Slats raised the guns, put the ring and pole sight on the bottom of the cowling, and sent two bursts into it. Fire immediately belched from the engine and the right wing dropped, then it descended in an ever-tightening spiral down into the undercast. Slats watched it all the way, saw no parachute, and assumed that he had killed the pilot.

Soon after that, all of the fighters disappeared and they were alone in the German sky, and at an altitude Slats estimated to be five thousand feet. Looking back alongside the tail wheel, he could see that the gunners were gone—he could not see Gaby lying on the floor—and up in the cockpit, he could see the elbows of both Fridgen and Waller. He still did not know about the burning engine, which soon fell off the wing. After waiting awhile to see if more fighters would be attacking, he decided to go up where he could man the top turret. So he began to crawl, pushing his left leg forward, then dragging his right leg up to it with the help of his wounded right hand. It was slow progress getting by the retracted tail wheel, and then he saw Gaby. He says that he saw the abdominal wound but did not look closely at it. And he did not stop because Gaby was screaming at him to get out, get out, get out. Getting through the bomb bay on the narrow catwalk was a trial, but by putting his bad leg on top of his good left leg, and by partially lifting himself with his hands, he was finally able to get across the catwalk and then collapsed on the floor behind the pilots. After lying there a minute, he reached up, touched Waller's arm to get his attention, then yelled that Gaby was in the back with a bad wound. Waller immediately left the cockpit, retrieved a morphine syringe to treat Gaby, then saw that Slats was holding his right leg and in pain. "Here, I'll give you a shot first," he said, bending over Slats.

"No, I'll be all right, go back and help Gaby."

"I'm going to give you a shot first," Waller replied and then inserted the needle in Slats's leg through the hole in his pants. Then he got another syringe and headed back through the bomb bay.

Slats just sat on the floor, his back propped up on the frame that held the top turret, and he thinks that Fridgen kept the airplane flying for nearly an hour. What he did not know at the time was that the second engine died, they flew on one and four for a while, then they both died. Slats realized what had happened, of course, because of the silence. Then he remembers seeing Palmer coming out of the nose and dropping out through the escape hatch. Shortly after that, he heard Fridgen say, "It just fits," and then they skidded to a crash landing.

First came the loud noise as the plane hit the ground and skidded, then there was a loud metallic sound as the scraping of the ball turret caused the back half of the fuselage to tear off and go spinning ahead of them. Slats had braced himself against the top turret frame and when they came to a stop, he started to move to test his body, and realized that he had survived without further damage. Fridgen immediately got out of his seat, limping because one of the rudder pedals had hit his ankle, then asked Slats if he knew whether or not Reilly had destroyed the secret radio. Slats claimed no knowledge of it, then Fridgen went back to the radio room and returned saying that it had not been destroyed but that he had taken care of it. He then checked to see if Slats was all right, and left saying that he was going to try to escape before soldiers or police arrived. Slats, realizing that there was no way he could follow, slowly inched his way out of the front fuselage, and as he dropped to the ground, he was surprised to find himself in about two inches of snow.

Then he looked in front of the fuselage where he had been, saw the back half about fifty yards away, and for some reason felt that he had to crawl there and retrieve the pair of brogans that he stashed just forward of his tunnel. He thinks he must have crawled about twenty yards when he heard a man's voice screaming at him. He turned and saw two German soldiers, one yelling at him, the other working the bolt of his rifle. He stopped immediately, sat up, and raised his hands. He had fear now because the German soldier was aiming the rifle at him. Soon, other soldiers arrived, then two French prisoner-laborers from the farm where they had landed came and carried him to a barn, where they laid him on the floor. He thinks he may have laid there for fifteen or twenty minutes before another two soldiers arrived. One of them then walked up to him, and with hate burning in his eyes, drew his right leg back and kicked Slats's wounded right knee as hard as he could with his steel-toed boot. Then, fearing the worst, Slats saw him draw back his leg again, but before he could kick him a second time, the other soldier grabbed his arm, pulled him back, and said something to him. At this time Slats knew nothing about Dante's *Inferno*, but if he had, he would now know that he had just been welcomed into the second circle of hell.

## CHAPTER 9

## Prisoner Patient

The farm where Homing Pigeon ended its service in the war had a bunkhouse where several French prisoners of war (POWs) stayed when they were not doing forced labor. After Slats received his brutal welcome to the POW class on the floor of the barn, two of those French laborers carried him to this bunkhouse and placed him on one of the cots. Minutes later, two other Frenchmen, one on each side, helped Lieutenant Ehmann walk into the bunkhouse. Slats, who had his eyes closed, immediately sat up and was shocked to hear the language that was flowing from his navigator. "He was using every swear word I'd ever heard and a bunch I had never heard," Slats said, remembering that poignant moment. But besides Ehmann's raving anger at the German SOBs that shot them down, what made it both memorable and terrible was the horror that Slats experienced when he looked at the face that was making the sounds. Ehmann's right eye was out of its socket and hanging down on his cheek, and when he sat down on his bed, Slats could see a deep gash in the right side of his skull. "I don't know if his brain was exposed or not; I was too horrified to look any more."

Somebody must have called for an ambulance because one showed up within a short time. "It looked just like one of our ambulances," Slats said. "It had two stretchers, one for each of us." The ambulance took them to the nearby town of Unna and to the little Catholic hospital there. They took Ehmann to surgery first, where they cleaned up his eye and treated his head wound. When the nuns brought him back to the ward, his head and the whole left side of his face was bandaged. Then they took Slats in and he happened to notice a clock saying that it was exactly nine o'clock. There, Slats was introduced to a Dr. Kuse, along with two or three nurses who were waiting to lay Slats on a surgery table. But Slats rose up despite the two nurses trying to hold him down. Then he looked at the doctor, made slicing motions with his hand just above the right knee. Then Doctor Kuse "gave me one of the warmest smiles I have ever seen and then shook his head." Slats, of course, was terribly afraid they were going to amputate his leg—that was his signal to the doctor—and he was greatly relieved to discover that was not going to happen. Then they pulled off his flight GI pants and long johns and examined his leg wounds. The wounds on the left thigh were minor and through one of the nurses who spoke English, the doctor explained that the small pieces of shrapnel would soon work their way out and he would not do any cutting. But when he examined the right leg, he called for a syringe with a long needle and injected an anesthetic that immediately numbed the area around the wound. Soon the doctor was cutting and probing, but Slats could only barely feel the doctor's fingers. Sometime later, the doctor showed him five pieces of shrapnel that, while he was on his knees behind his guns, had entered the leg and gone under his kneecap. "It was one big hole, I'll tell you, and I didn't find out until it started healing that it was actually two holes side by side with skin and muscle in between."

Then, when he was back in one of the hospital beds, the nurse who spoke English and the doctor came to his bedside. In quiet speech—Ehmann was in the next room—the doctor spoke to the nurse, who then translated. He explained that he had done everything he could with the head wound, but that there was steel in there that could not be removed and it had caused a huge blood clot to form. Then he said, with a real sad expression on his face, that sometime that clot was going to break and it would all be over. Ehmann was not going to make it, but the doctor wanted Slats to know that he had done the best that he could to save Ehmann's life.

Slats thinks he was able to sleep that night, and the next morning he clearly remembers what they brought him for breakfast. It was a loaf of black bread "that looked like it weighed about twelve ounces, but when I lifted it, it felt like it weighed seven pounds. And it was covered with sawdust and made out of potatoes. Black brut, they called it. Then I tasted it, and it tasted worse than anything I had ever eaten. But, the funny thing is, I wouldn't eat it for two days, but on the third day I was so hungry it tasted like chocolate."

Right after their "breakfast," another ambulance took Ehmann and Slats fifteen miles south of Unna to a bigger hospital in the small city of Hemer. There, they put the two of them in a large room together. Soon afterward, when a doctor examined Slats's knee, a technician of some kind came in the room, helped Slats "cock" his leg—bend it halfway—then attached a steel brace that would keep his leg in that position. And to take some of the pressure off the knee, pillows were stuffed under his knee to hold up the leg.

All the while, Ehmann, in the bed next to him, "was extremely coherent and did a lot of talking. He again thanked me for taking such good care of his guns, then he told about a short round that he had when the fighters were attacking—he said he kept firing, sighting with his good eye, after he was wounded. Then he would talk about his nice wife who was down in North Florida, and how, when he got back, he was just going to sit around and drink that wonderful Florida orange juice. Also, he knew he had a baby son, but there wasn't anything about him he knew enough to talk about. It was really sad for me to hear him talk about going home because I had believed what Dr. Kuse told me—I felt certain he knew what he was talking about."

While Slats was confined to his bed, he remembers two things happening. First, a Lieutenant Moody and another flyer whose name he has forgotten were brought into the room. But their injuries were minor, and they soon were taken away. The other thing he remembers was that he made a new "friend of sorts." This was a Russian prisoner who had been working in a mine but who had come down with an ear infection. And apparently he was so good working with patients that they kept him as an orderly. Every day, he came to Slats, gave him what Slats calls a "spit bath," and shaved him regularly. He was called Panoff and appeared to be quite intelligent because he was constantly bugging the Americans for English words that he could learn. "I remember, I taught him the word 'door' and he went to our door, pounded on it, and said, 'Door! Door! Door!' He called me Mr. Brown because my face had so many freckles. Then one day, they kicked him out of our room—he wasn't supposed to be speaking English, but you know what? He was back the next day and he kept coming back. Also, he thought all Americans were rich. He would say, 'Mr. Brown, you rich, everybody rich in America'—he had a list of names—Rockefeller, Dupont, etc. I told him not all of us are rich, that some are poor, and that I had a poor family, then he would reply, 'No, no, no, Mr. Brown, you rich, you rich.'"

Two weeks passed, then on March 8, with just the two of them in the room, it happened. Slats heard groaning in the bed next to him. He rolled over to look at Ehmann, who was sitting straight up, and then he saw blood pouring out of his mouth. Slats watched in horror as his head then slumped, with his body still in the sitting position. Ehmann died in just that short time. Slats yelled and someone came in and laid Ehmann down, then a bit later they carried the body out on a stretcher. Slats thinks it was a day or two later when some male orderlies carried him to the hospital window where they pointed out Ehmann's grave below them. Those were sad, sad days for prisoner patient Slayton.

Slats thinks they took his brace off on March 27, and that he left the next day on a train, accompanied by one guard, that would take him to Frankfurt. It was a night train and Slats slept most of the way, consequently he did not get to see much of the countryside. But he saw two things when he reached the busy train station the next morning that shocked him. The first was the bomb damage. "It was just incredible—this was the first time I had ever seen what bombs could do. I know we tried not to bomb business and residential areas, but I'm sure we were guilty for some of what I saw." The second thing that greatly impressed him was the people and the way they treated him. They knew he was an American by his GI uniform and everywhere he looked, people were glaring at him angrily. "I have never seen such hate in people's faces," he said, shaking his head. They also yelled at him—probably curses—and he thinks he was spit on several times. Luckily, his guard, "an older gentleman, was a pretty decent fellow and I think a couple of times he had to use his arms to restrain some of them. And, to tell you the truth, after seeing all of that damage, not only at the station, but also, while riding in the back of a truck, through the city to the hospital about three miles out of the city, I didn't blame them for being angry. I would probably have been angry, too, if I had lived through what they did."

The place where they took him was Dalag Luft, which was both a POW hospital and the Luftwaffe's main interrogation center. There, using a combination of tiny, solitary-confinement cells to scare and intimidate downed aviators, along with lavish dining rooms where high-ranking officers and potential collaborators could be entertained, the goal of the English-speaking interrogation staff was to extract and assemble every tiny bit of information that could help the Luftwaffe's cause. Many accounts have been written about the experiences American and British airmen had with this staff. And Slats's experiences were in most ways typical. He was placed in a solitary cell for a day, maybe a day and a half. Then he was escorted to an office and seated in front of a desk, where he was interrogated by an English-speaking officer. Of course, Slats, like all his fellow airmen, had been taught that the rules of the Geneva Convention governing prisoners state that a prisoner only has to give his name, rank, and serial number. That was what he did, and then "this real bright young man" gave him a paper and pencil with questions on it, he just made a big X, and signed his name. But then the interrogating officer smiled and began asking him questions about his crew. Slats gave the standard reply, name, rank, and serial number, which seemed to amuse his interrogator. Finally, still smiling, the officer read from a paper, telling Slats that his pilot was 1st Lt. Francis Fridgen, his copilot was 2nd Lt. David Waller, and so on down the line, with every name and rank complete and accurate. Slats was greatly impressed, of course, but so was every other airman who has passed on an account of his visit to the center. They were all treated to detailed information about their crew or their squadron or their airplane. "I just assumed that some member of my crew had already talked to them," Slats said. "I don't know how else they could have gotten that information." That same kind of statement, in one form or another, accompanied most of the other accounts that have been read by the author.

What happened after that was probably not typical. After getting his POW number, 52285, he was taken to a room that was completely darkened. And as he entered, the stench almost made him sick. Then as he struggled to climb into an upper bunk—the guard, probably to cause him agony from his injured leg, insisted that Slats had to climb up without help—he thought that he was going to throw up because of the foul odor that filled the room. The guard then closed the door and Slats, not knowing what was going to happen to him, laid there in pain and tried to think how he could blot out the sickening stench and get some sleep. Just as he was finally drifting off, he felt a hand touching him. Startled, he quickly opened his eyes and stared into the dark. Then he was able to see a pair of swollen eyes and some lips. "It scared the living hell out of me, and the guy smelled so bad it was incredible. Then I realized, when I could see a little more of his face, that he had a black nose, and that what I was smelling was burnt flesh. All the guy wanted was some help. He asked me if I would point him toward the door, that he had to go to the bathroom. I did that, and when he opened the door, I could see another guy lying in a bunk. The one who came to me talked like an Englishman so I assumed they were both crewmen who had escaped a bomber that had been on fire. We always heard, whether it was right or not, that the Lancaster and the Short Sterling were quick to burn. Luckily, they came and got me the next morning and was I ever happy to get out there and get away from that stench. Burnt flesh has a horrible odor."

In the truck on the way to the train station, Slats was told that they were going to Obermassfeld, which was an orthopedic hospital just over five miles south of the city of Meiningen. He was also told that it was run by British POWs, most of whom were captured at Dunkirk early in the war. When they got on the train, Slats "buddied up" with two amputees and he still remembers their names: Dusty Kester and Luther Smith. "Dusty was from the Chicago area and Smitty was from Maine. I got pretty close to Smitty later. He had lost his left arm."

Slats remembers little of the train trip, except that they made lots of stops while other trains passed them by. But he does remember arriving at the hospital, which was called a lazarette. "It was a big three-story building and with one crutch, I had to hop and skip to get up and down the stairs."

At the time he arrived at this lazarette, Slats could not bend his leg at all—it was like it was permanently fixed in the cocked position the way it had been in the brace. The purpose of his internment there was to change that and immediately, along with a Canadian whose last name was Cockeday, who had toes that could not be bent, a man who may or may not have been trained in physical therapy started to work on their problems. And Slats vividly remembers the pain they both suffered. "The guy's name was Albert and he was an Englishman, and he would come to our room every day and work on me one day and Cockeday the next. He would take a hold of my leg and forcefully straighten or bend it. It was terribly painful and I held my fist in my mouth to keep from crying out. But my problem wasn't as bad as Cockeday's. He could not move a toe on either foot, so Albert would just start moving them up and down while Cockeday held one fist in his mouth and tried to climb the bed post with the other. It became a routine; I'd watch him suffer one day and he would watch me suffer the next. But it worked. I always felt better after Albert worked me over and Cockeday I think did, too. Then one day another guy came in named Grant with a leg problem. He would watch us go through treatments and could see the pain suffered by Cockeday when Albert would wiggle his toes as fast as he could—oh, how he suffered. Anyway, we kept telling Grant that he had better get out and start walking or he would have to suffer when Albert started on him. The next day, Grant left and we saw him out the window, walking around a little circle, and by golly he got his leg loosened up enough that he never had to go through what we did."

Slats went through the therapy for over a month and by then was able to get up and down the stairs without his crutch. He still had some pain when he bent his leg, but Albert told him to keep moving it as much as he could and the pain would eventually go away. There was really no formal discipline at this hospital so Slats took every opportunity to walk around, visiting other rooms and chatting with the other patients. On one of these rounds he saw Smitty, one of his two buddies on the train ride, and he was trying to cook some extra potatoes that he had somehow gotten. Slats saw him struggling, trying to cut or peel them with just his right hand, so he went over to help him. Smitty immediately objected. "Slayton, don't help me anymore because I've got to learn to do things myself." Then he explained that he was soon to be repatriated and did not know whether he would be fitted with a hook for his left arm. Then he apologized, saying something like,

"Don't misunderstand, I appreciate what you tried to do—it's just that I'm going to have to get through life this way and I don't want to be dependent on somebody else for things I can learn to do by myself."

Slats also remembers another amputee that was even more fiercely independent than Smitty. "We had a guy—he was from Cincinnati, Ohio—who bailed out of a bomber and his chute got caught on the horizontal stabilizer and got torn. This caused him to fall too fast and when he hit, he broke both legs. After that he crawled for three days and was real thirsty when he came to a stream. So he crawled down the bank to get a drink, then fell in, and with his broken legs, couldn't get out. He kept hollering for help and finally some farmer heard him and pulled him out of the stream. But he was in there a long time and after he got out, one of his arms was paralyzed. When they brought him to our hospital, they had to amputate both of his legs, and one arm was almost useless. But it didn't bother him a bit. He rode around in his wheelchair, cheering everybody up, and telling everybody how lucky he was to be alive. Then one day, a guy came who had severed an artery in one leg, was bleeding badly, and they were going to amputate his leg. He refused, and then they had this guy from Cincinnati come talk to him. When he did, he swore at him and called him a dumb, rotten son-of-a-bitch if he was going to let himself die—I didn't hear this, I got it second hand. But it worked, the guy allowed them to do the surgery. And I said to myself, 'Slayton, quit feeling sorry for yourself. You're all in one piece; just get with it and exercise; keep that leg moving and forget the pain.'"

A little later, Albert felt Slats's leg go all the way back and announced that he couldn't do any more for him—that he had to keep exercising if he wanted the leg to work properly. And that triggered the end of his stay at Obermassfeld.

# CHAPTER 10

## Stalag Luft VI

Slats has lost track of the dates and time he spent at the Obermassfeld lazerette, but thinks it was about six weeks. He also thinks it was a little past mid-May when he, along with about eight other recovering patients—some from the smaller lazerette in Meiningen just a few miles north of them, were escorted to the train station by two guards. There, they boarded a train that would start them on a trip to Hydekrug, East Prussia (now Silute, Lithuania), where a large POW camp housed downed NCO airmen from the British Empire and United States. The name of the camp was Stalag Luft VI, and it was run by officers of the Luftwaffe instead of the Gestapo or the SS personnel who ran the concentration camps and who engineered the Holocaust. Slats remembers little about the trip except for a coal and water stop in Magdeburg, which from his train window "looked like a beautiful city not yet bombed [that would happen in September], and I remember two beautiful, big highways intersecting, one going east and west and the other north and south." But, for him at least, the whole train ride was a frightening experience and he explains why. "Our orders were always, if you can't drop your bombs over the assigned target, do your best to drop them on any kind of train that you see. Also, trains were a favorite target of our escorting fighters. So, especially in the daylight hours, I was worried that we might get bombed or strafed."

And what is his memory of arriving at the POW camp? "It looked old and run down, like it hadn't been taken care of. Somehow I got the idea that it was built during World War I, but I was later told that it was built in 1939 and first used for Polish prisoners." Slats was lucky to be assigned to a room in one of the brick buildings rather than in one of the hastily built wooden barracks or in the tent city that had been created to house the estimated nine thousand airmen the Germans had sent there.

As he walked by one of the fences that separated the quarters, he heard a sound that he was hoping to hear: Sergeant Brennan, the flight engineer and top turret gunner in his crew, yelled loudly, "There's Slayton!" Slats had been thinking on the whole trip there that he might get to see the four gunners who had bailed out when their third engine was on fire. And, on his first day, there were all four of them: Brennan, Bartle, Reilly, and Abernathy at the fence. Later, he would see them "two or three times," but the experiences were a little bit of a letdown. "They had made new friends in their barracks and they had been with some of them almost three months—also, they were quite a ways from me. What hurt the most was that they weren't even interested in my story, although they did listen when I told them what happened to Ehmann. But this was a prison camp and I soon learned that one really has to look after those closest to you, and this creates pretty strong bonds. So, while I was a bit hurt, I also understood their situation and didn't hold it against them."

Slats was placed in a room with nine other kriegies, and it was adjacent to the other room in the barracks building where ten others were housed. Within a short time, he learned that he and his nine roommates were what they called a "combine," which was a group that shared food and cooking chores for the one meal a day they had to prepare for themselves. The good news was that they received regular Red Cross food parcels that were a welcome delight after suffering their one-meal-a-day bowl, typically slimy barley soup, perhaps with a piece of horsemeat fat in it, and often with floating white worms (probably fly or beetle larvae)—worms that were highly prized by the long-term prisoners who realized that their bodies were hurting for protein. Each man shared one of the parcels with his food mate, who, in Slats's case, was a young man named Russell Schlyer from Cincinnati, Ohio, and who became a very good friend. After a bit of prompting, Slats then remembered the names of some others in the room with him, or in the adjacent room, a feat that seems remarkable considering that sixty-seven years had passed. But, here, besides Schlyer, are the names:

Nicholas Mucci, a cocky little guy from Newark, New Jersey

Thomas K. Hora, who bragged about all his lady friends, from Louisville, Kentucky

Francis Harnish, from Greenfield, Massachusetts

Nicholas Bengler, a guy as nice as he was big, from St. Louis, Missouri

Charles Deckert Jr., from Ozone, New York

Tommy Laspata, always full of mischief, from New York City

Melvin "Pop" Brown, much older, a real nice man, skillful hand printer, from West Palm Beach, Florida

Jablonski, left handed, could really spike a Ping-Pong ball, from Pittsburgh, Pennsylvania

Klingkowski, Slats's Ping-Pong partner, from Pennsylvania

Slats immediately learned that there were two patterns of behavior most of the prisoners exhibited. First, there was the routine behavior. This was the wake-up, then the walk to the end of the building to urinate against a brick wall with a sloping drain at the bottom. Then, there was the wait until six o'clock—in their Germanic way the guards were usually very punctual—when their door was unlocked. Then it was a walk to a slit trench with about forty sit-down facilities where they could relieve themselves, followed by a wash-up at a place for that. Then it was *Appell*, the morning roll call where they would stand in formation—some survivors say that they stood at attention, but Slats insists that they just stood in a relaxed posture while two guards would walk in front of them, counting.

The other type of behavior was what prisoners did to break the monotony—behavior that would bring stimulation and physical challenges into their dull lives. For Slats, this began right after the body count, and his knee injury was the stimulus. "I knew I had to exercise my knee or I'd end up being a cripple. So I talked to my partner, Russell, who had a limp—he had hurt his ankle some way—and I said that I was going to start running every day. He thought that was a good idea, so that is what we did. We started running around the inside of our laager, well inside the warning wire, and I'm guessing that we probably did two miles every morning. At first my knee was really hurting, but I was never tempted to stop. I just did not want to be a twenty-year-old cripple."

After that, it became Slats's duty to slice the loaf of black brut that they were issued—slice it into ten pieces that would be shared with his combine. (One day he cut a finger badly with the makeshift knife that one of the guys had made out of a can opener—the cut healed without getting infected.) Then, he utilized three more options that would bring some stimulation into his day.

One option was to play Ping-Pong on the big table that they had in their barracks—the paddles and balls had been supplied by the Red Cross or the American USO. "I got pretty good at that—in fact, Jablonski, a left hander, was the only one I couldn't beat—boy, could he spike that ball. I also played a lot of doubles with Klingkowski—I can't remember his first name."

The second option was to join the ongoing poker game. "We used cards supplied by the Red Cross, and the money was the cigarettes we received in our packets. I lost a lot when I first started because I didn't know a damn thing about five-card stud, or seven-card stud, or five-card draw, or seven-card high-low. I bet foolishly sometimes just out of ignorance, but, you know what? I didn't smoke so it was no big loss, but the main thing was that, by watching the mistakes others made, I really learned how to play poker, and before too long, I was a constant winner. How much did we bet? I can't remember ever seeing a bet of more than five cigarettes, and that didn't happen very often."

The third option was also a new one for him. "I had never been much of a reader—oh, I remember the painful experience I had in high school with Miss Schmidt, who made us read *Silas Mariner*. That was boring as hell and I hated it. Then she would make us read an essay every Friday. I remember

I was supposed to be reading an essay by an anthropologist, "Apology for Man," but I sat back there reading the school newspaper, and I really caught hell. She didn't like me and I didn't think much of her. She was the only teacher in my years at school that I ever had any trouble with. Anyhow, here I am with hours to kill, not considering myself a reader, and I see some of the other guys reading books. So, since I have a big supply of cigarettes to trade, I thought, what the hell; I started trading for some of them, and, before long, I got hooked on reading. Pop Brown, who was really good at hand printing, wrote the names of the books I read in the little hymn book one of the chaplains gave me—a book I still have. This is a list of forty-six books, including eight Erle Stanley Gardner mysteries. But my favorite was Lloyd C. Douglas's *Disputed Passage*." (Not all the forty-six books were read in Stalag Luft VI—he and Pop Brown would stick together under different circumstances.)

Other diversions were exercised by many of the kriegies. One was softball, and there is a good story to go with that. Thanks to the Red Cross, a shipment of softballs was sent to the camp—bats were not allowed because they could be weapons, so the men fashioned bats out of other wooden materials they could find. Slats and his roommates did not know—a fact that was revealed later—that the camp leaders were sending out letters to relatives that had hidden code messages that the censors could not decipher. One of the requests that went out was for parts to make a small radio with which they could pick up BBC short-wave broadcasts from London. Some innovative intelligence man or woman came up with the idea of smuggling the necessary parts for building such a radio inside softballs that were to be shipped. And it worked. With these parts, along with a part or two they got after bribing a guard, they were soon receiving the news broadcasts and spreading the news around the camp. This is how they found out about the D-Day invasion on June 6 while, at the same time, German propagandists in the camp were telling the kriegies that an attempted invasion of France had been stopped and the American enemy destroyed. All Slats knew was that, when they received the softballs they were to play with, all of them were partially unsewed and had to be resewed before they could be used.

Boxing was another diversion made possible by two factors. One was that there were a number of men who had been professional boxers in the camp. Two, most of the men had grown up when prize fighting was a huge sport in America, where every schoolboy past the fourth grade could relate the details of the famous match where the German, Max Schmeling, knocked out the American heavyweight champion, Joe Lewis. And thousands of these schoolboys went on to train as amateur boxers in the nationwide Golden Gloves Program—a program for youth who aspired to become professional boxers. Consequently, some of these aspirants were among the nine thousand or so who ended up incarcerated in Stalag Luft VI and who were eager to continue with the sport.

All this ties in with a significant event in Slats's life as a prisoner in the camp. One day, while the men were milling around outside, Slats somehow got in a conversation with a gunner who had been on a B-24 crew. The B-24 had some similarities with the B-17: it had four engines, could carry as much or more of a bomb load, and was heavily armed, bristling with .50 caliber machine guns in turrets and other positions. But, it had a narrow Davis wing that was more susceptible to flak damage and fires that would erupt when the tanks were pierced with hot shrapnel. Also, it had a lower service ceiling, which, in turn, exposed it more to the flak that was heavy over most targets. Now, picture Slats and the B-24 gunner, a much bigger man, in their conversation. At first, it was just that, conversation. Then the conversation became heated, morphed into an argument, and this was followed by a loss of temper on the part of the B-24 gunner. "Suddenly, he took a swing at me, which I saw coming and ducked from, then he took another swing and I ducked that. By then, I was angry and I let go with a right that got him on the chin, and then I sent one into his stomach. He went away after that."

But then the story gets better. It just so happened that the most famous American boxer in the camp, a man whose name was Steve Swidirski, but who was much better known as the Bearded Marvel because of his heavy black beard, was there to see the exchange. After the B-24 gunner went on his way, Swidirski came up to Slats and said, "Hey, for a little squirt, you did a pretty good job with that guy. I liked the way you were able to duck his punches—I'd like to get you in the ring and show you some stuff. I can get a kid your size and, with me helping you, I think you could become a good boxer." At first Slats told him that he did not think he wanted to do that, but with Swidirski's persistence, Slats finally agreed to meet him at the ring where they practiced. "I went and put on the gloves—I suppose the Red Cross or the USO must have brought them—and got in the ring with this guy. I started punching him with my right hand and we were going at it pretty good when Swidirski stopped us and asked me: 'Are you left handed?' I said, 'No,' and he said that if I was right handed, I should be punching with my left, then swinging with my stronger right arm." Slats can't remember much else, except that he had no interest in learning how to box and that he did not go back for more of the Bearded Marvel's instruction.

However, there is a footnote to this story. The kriegies were wild about staging a camp championship fight between the

Americans versus the British Empire boxers mainly from Canada, Australia, and Great Britain. So, with approval of the camp commandant, a "strict and militarily formal Prussian officer who was also very fair and followed the Geneva Convention regulations to the letter," the big date was set for July 14, a date by which all of the preliminary lead-up bouts would be over. Slats well remembers the day when most of the thousands gathered on each side of the wire separating the two major contingencies, all of them betting wildly on the outcomes of the championship fights. Slats insists that he was not one of them. "I really did not have much interest. Besides, there were so many crowded out there, you couldn't really see what was happening in the ring. But, I do remember that the Bearded Marvel beat this Aussie guy and won the heavyweight championship."

Another diversion that Slats had no interest in was an escape attempt. And, yes, he knew that it was his duty to try to escape—that had been hammered into them back in England before they started flying missions. "But it made no sense to me. Where could you go, to Russia?" However, despite Slats's lack of interest, numerous accounts of escape attempts have been recorded, one that details how one of the escapees was discovered and shot by a guard. And although a few managed to break out of the camp for a while, the author is unaware of any who were not eventually captured.

Slats has one other story of a brain-stimulating barracks caper:

There was this guy in our barracks by the name of Tommy Laspata from New York City who announced one day: "I'm going to kill me a German shepherd and I need some help." See, even if you were the most ardent dog lover, you would still hate the guard dogs they had trained; they were savage beasts. Well, Tommy got a couple of the guys to help him. Their job was to get up in the rafters and hold the heavy shutters up while Tommy teased one of the dogs that was always patrolling outside after lockup. Well, he did that—he teased one of the dogs, who came at him, lunging through the window. Just then, Tommy yelled, "Drop it!" and the shutters crashed down on the dog's neck, killing it. Then they threw it back out into the laager, and Tommy said, "Let's do it again."

So they did it again, and this time the dog had almost leaped all the way through the window when the shutters caught his back, leaving only his rear and hind legs sticking out the window. Tommy, who was holding the shutters down as the dog cried and moaned, said, "Now what are we going to do?" One of the guys said, "We'll get him out and we're going to tear up your bed in order to do it." Then they took his blanket, held it under the front part of the dog while those on the rafters lifted the shutters off. Then, they lifted the dog with the blanket and got him back out the window and into the laager. This just shows you what guys will do when they are bored. One more thing about Tommy—he bailed out when one of their engines caught fire, but then it went out, the others stayed in and returned, and he was afraid that he would be charged for being AWOL [absent without leave] if he was ever liberated. And I have no idea what happened. I don't know if he even survived.

Stalag Luft VI had been a miserable existence for all the men—many had dysentery, tuberculosis, and other diseases that the camp doctor could not even begin to treat. But within days after the biggest event in the camp, the championship boxing matches, many of the kriegies would descend into the next circle of hell. And Slats would be one of them.

1. At age fifteen, Slats caddied for Walt
Clemens, a member of the Fargo Country
Club. Submitted by Lowell E. Slayton from
personal collection.

2. Eighteen-year-old Slats
on the day he received his
uniform before heading to
Missouri for basic training.
Submitted by Lowell E. Slayton
from personal collection.

3. This portrait was a gift from
Slats to his mother before he
shipped out. Submitted by
Lowell E. Slayton from
personal collection.

4. Fridgen's Pigeons (*from left to right*): (*back row*) Brennan, Abernathy, Reilly, Bartle, Gaby, and Slats; (*front row*) Fridgen, Waller, Ehmann, and Palmer. Submitted by Lowell E. Slayton from personal collection.

5. Slats's plane after it was shot down on February 22, 1944. The inner starboard engine has ripped off its mountings in the crash and the Plexiglas nose cone has been completely smashed. Reproduced by permission of the Bundesarchiv, Koblenz.

6. The tail unit of the B-17, carrying the black "L" in a white triangle marking of the 381st Bomb Group. As the tail gunner, Slats was sitting in this section of the plane when one of the mortar rockets hit the fuselage behind him, creating an eighteen-inch-wide hole. Reproduced by permission of the Bundesarchiv, Koblenz.

7. Twisted propeller blades on the port engines of the plane indicate that both were turning when the B-17 made its final landing about three miles south of Unna at Ostendorf. Reproduced by permission of the Bundesarchiv, Koblenz.

# WESTERN (11)
# UNION

A. N. WILLIAMS
PRESIDENT

SYMBOLS

DL = Day Letter
NL = Night Letter
LC = Deferred Cable
NLT = Cable Night Letter
Ship Radiogram

MA510 46 GOVT=WUX WASHINGTON DC 8 644P    1944 MAR 8 PM 6 17

MRS CHRISTINE SLAYTON=

911 FIRST AVE SOUTH FARGO NDAK=

THE SECRETARY OF WAR DESIRES ME TO EXPRESS HIS DEEP REGRET
THAT YOUR SON STAFF SERGEANT LOWELL E SLAYTON HAS BEEN
REPORTED MISSING IN ACTION SINCE TWENTY TWO FEBRUARY OVER
GERMANY PERIOD IF FUTTHER DETAILS OR OTHER INFORMATION ARE
RECIVEDYOU WILL BE PROMPTLY NOTIFIED PERIOD=

ULIO THE ADJUTANT GENERAL.

THE COMPANY WILL APPRECIATE SUGGESTIONS FROM ITS PATRONS CONCERNING ITS SERVICE

# WESTERN (19)
# UNION

A. N. WILLIAMS
PRESIDENT

SYMBOLS

DL = Day Letter
NL = Night Letter
LC = Deferred Cable
NLT = Cable Night Letter
Ship Radiogram

MA60A 38 GOVT=WASHINGTON DC 5 654P    1944 MAR 5 PM 6 44

MRS CHRISTINE SLAYTON=

911 FIRST AVE SOUTH FARGO=

REPORT JUST RECEIVED THROUGH THE INTERNATIONAL RED CROSS
STATES THAT YOUR SON STAFF SERGEANT LOWELL E SLAYTON IS A
PRISONER OF WAR OF THE GERMAN GOVERNMENT REPORT FURTHER STATES
WOUNDED LETTER OF INFORMATION FOLLOWS FROM PROVOST MARSHAL
GENERAL=

DUNLOP ACTING THE ADJUTANT GENERAL.

THE COMPANY WILL APPRECIATE SUGGESTIONS FROM ITS PATRONS CONCERNING ITS SERVICE

8. (*opposite*) Two telegrams received by Slats's mother, the first telling her that Slats had been missing in action since February 22, 1944, and the second explaining that he was now a prisoner of war. Submitted by Lowell E. Slayton from personal collection.

9. Zella O. Pelloux, future Mrs. Slayton (*right*), and Gladys A. Jedlicka both served in the Women's Army Corps during the war. This photograph was taken in San Francisco for a recruiting/marketing campaign. Submitted by Lowell E. Slayton from personal collection.

10. The view from Slats's room at Hospital Katharine in Unna. He was soon moved to a hospital in Hemer, where he stayed until he was well enough to go to prison camp. Submitted by Lowell E. Slayton from personal collection.

11. (*opposite*) Diagram of Stalag Luft IV, a prisoner-of-war camp in Gross Tychow, Pomerania (now Gmina Tychowo, Poland). Submitted by Lowell E. Slayton from personal collection.

# Stalag Luft IV

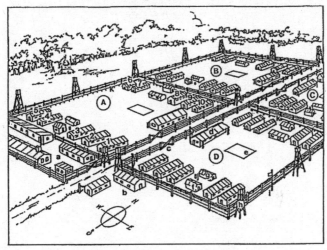

I was in A lager in barracks 9

A,B,C,D,————— compounds or lagers - divided into four self-contained units.

1————10————— barracks, 10 in each lager, approximately 40x130 ft. containing 10 rooms, designed for 16 men but reached overflowing capacity of 33 men per room

a————vorlager————— vorlager, an outer camp housing the German administration buildings, hospital and quarters for German personnel

b————warehouses— Red Cross parcels were stored there

c————entrance gate to each lager—just a way in

d————kitchen?— contained—2 offices, 2 sleeping rooms and a general purpose room

e————fire pool————— shallow concrete pool filled with rain water and became stagnant & mosquito infested

f————wash house———— with an abundant supply of cold water

g————latrine————————a place that was constantly occupied, a place where rumors were born

h————guard tower— manned, 24 hours a day with trigger happy Nazis

i————search light— to aid the trigger happy Nazis at night

j————water pump— situated in close proximity to the latrine

k————guard rail————— a wooden rail 2 feet high, it encompassed 3 sides of the lager and read, "Anyone touching this rail will be shot."

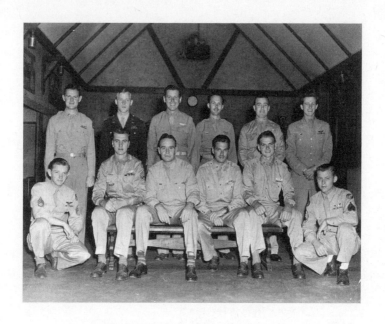

12. Slats with fellow North Dakota
prisoners of war, taken after returning
home. Submitted by Lowell E. Slayton
from personal collection.

# CHAPTER 11

## Deeper into the Inferno

In early July there were rumors flying everywhere in Stalag Luft VI. From their secret radio, parts of which were carried by ten different kriegies and assembled quickly when in a secure location, they knew that the Soviets had an offensive launched toward them and the Baltic. The rumors dealt with different views on what was going to happen to them. One story was that the Germans would escape and leave them to be liberated by the Soviets. Another was that America was going to reward the Soviets an amount somewhere between five and fifty dollars for each American they saved. Others scoffed at both those stories, saying that Hitler needed them as bargaining chips, so the Germans would move them out to another camp.

Several of the kriegies have speculated that the German commandant, prior to the boxing championships, had probably received an order telling him what he was to do with the prisoners. But even though the word never got out, many of the kriegies began preparing for a move by sewing packs out of old shirts and other spare clothing that could be used to carry their possessions to wherever they would be sent. Slats remembers the rumors and that he sensed they were going to be moved, but he cannot remember any special preparations. What he does remember is that they had very little notice and that none of them were ready when the order came to move. According to a kriegie named Tom McHale who was asked by the camp leader, T.Sgt. Frank Paulus, to stay and leave with the last of the prisoners, "Relays of Germans had come into our deserted camp; first Luftwaffe guards and then Wehrmacht [army] guards from a nearby post. They scavenged abandoned barracks, picking up what the POWs had left. Here were members of the so-called master race mopping up behind American POWs" (from B24.net: Second Generation Research). Because of this, some kriegies have speculated that the short notice was deliberate so valuables would have to be left for scavenging.

Slats cannot remember the exact day they got orders to move, but another kriegie who kept a diary claims that it was about three p.m., Friday, July 14, when most of the American prisoners left the camp, boarded a train in Heydekrug, and were taken a short distance to the seacoast port of Memel. There, they were marched to the dock where they waited in line to board a captured Soviet collier (coal carrier) named the *Masuren*, which, Carter Lunsford, in a later account, said "still had the hammer and sickle on the funnel." When asked if he remembered that, Slats admitted that he did not, then said, "But I sure as hell remember what happened next."

The men boarded the ship, then stood in line to step into an open hatch, then descend on a ladder into the hold of the ship. Everybody was carrying what possessions they could, and in order to get down the ladder, they had to drop their belongings straight down, then descend and try to retrieve them. The huge problem was that there was no light in the hold and after a short time it was packed with men, making it difficult, if not impossible, for the arrivals to find their possessions. To add to the problem, one or more guards were at the foot of the ladder and when a kriegie got down, he was immediately shoved away so others could descend. Slats, along with his now close friend, Russ Schlyer, simply dropped whatever they did not have in their pockets or tied to their waists, descended the ladder, and were immediately shoved into the mass of standing bodies. "I was carrying two suits of clothes, one for me and one for Russ, and he was carrying two food parcels. We never were able to retrieve any of that."

Slats remembers that there was no question in his mind that he had descended into another level of hell. "The odor, which we smelled before we went down the ladder, was a heavy urine smell. Then, when we got down, it was so bad I thought I was going to puke. The stench of urine was just horrible. But, worse, was the heat. Remember, this was July and the temperature down there, with all those bodies, had to be over a hundred. Also, we were on the coast where the humidity was probably 100 percent. I mean, it was just minutes before the sweat was pouring off of us."

The ship left that evening—some think there were at least a thousand men in that hold. That number sounds high, but when asked, Slats thought there could have been more than that. He remembers that they were packed so tightly that he could maybe flex his knees an inch or so, and that there was definitely no one enjoying the leisure of sitting or lying down. Others have told similar stories and all of them conclude that everybody in the hold of that ship had to stand while they traveled.

According to another source, when the men finally debarked from the ship, a man named Delgado tried to raise the morale and take their minds off the torture by leading a songfest. Slats doesn't remember it, but admits that he could have forgotten it, "because I was definitely not a singer."

Another story relates how one British airman aboard said that he and other crews had dropped a lot of mines in the waters they would be going through—because of the advancing Soviets, they all assumed they were heading west and into Germany. After that, when they heard clinking sounds of metal hitting the hull, those around the airman heard him shout, "Get ready!" and then, after a moment when there was no explosion, he would say, "Well, we survived that one."

A more poignant story dealt with a more mundane matter: body elimination. How was it to be done in such a packed mass and with no toilet facilities? Eventually, for number one (younger readers may not know the standard polite terminology these men were taught to use for the two wastes: one was for liquid, two was for solid) the Germans dropped a large bucket through the hatch with a rope and it was passed around. Slats remembers a man standing by him named J. N. Blake receiving the bucket, which he used, then hearing him yell that nobody "can take a piss now because I filled it." Others started yelling for him to pass the bucket along so a guard at the ladder could take or hand it up. This advice worked, "although I don't know how they were able to pass it to him without spilling it."

Number two was a much more difficult problem. Those who could speak German passed the word around that the guards would let one man at a time go up the ladder and take care of the problem on deck. Slats clearly remembers that one man immediately pushed himself to the ladder, was given permission to go up, and then, after a few moments they all heard shots. "We found out later that the guy who went up was kind of a nut case and that he immediately went to the railing and jumped into the water. The shots we heard were the guards killing him."

According to one kriegie's diary, they departed the evening of July 14, traveled all night and all the next day, and arrived at the dock in Swinemünde (now Swinoujscie, Poland) in the "wee hours" of the morning on July 16. If that is correct, they were standing in that heat and foul air, with no water or food, for two nights and one day—about thirty-six hours. When asked how he was able to survive under those conditions, Slats could only give a lame answer. "You just tell yourself, 'If these guys can do it, so can I.'" When asked to give more details, he just shrugged and said, "The desire to live is pretty strong in a young man, and I figured I wouldn't live if I collapsed and was trampled in the dark by the others."

When the guards shouted for them to get out, Slats and Russ managed to climb the ladder and walk off the boat, but many had to be helped by sympathetic kriegies around them. Then, after they got into the line to the railroad cars that were waiting for them, they moved slowly forward and were eventually shoved and jammed into another sweat chamber where they learned that they would have to stay like this while they waited for another load of kriegies that were on the way. So, all day, in the hot sun and with very little water, they suffered in the railroad car.

While there, one kriegie, T.Sgt. Carter Lunsford, remembers: "The doors to the boxcars were open and we could see all the activities around us. . . . The siding was right beside a German battle cruiser, the *Prinz Eugene*. We watched all day long as the German sailors practiced their battle drills and they piped officers on and off the ship. Water was scarce and it was hot in there. . . . At some point in the late afternoon, Feldwebel Helmut Schroeder came to each car in its turn. He was the interpreter from Luft VI and by all accounts, a good man. He told us that the guards from Luft IV were coming to take charge and that we were all to be put in chains."

What none of the kriegies knew at the time was that there had been a major change in the administration and management policies for the Luftwaffe camps. According to historians who have commented on these changes, they were caused by the Great Escape, the historic breakout of seventy-three kriegies from Stalag Luft III—a story that has been filmed and written about, but the success of which was brief and tragic—seventy of the seventy-three escapees were recaptured and fifty were immediately executed. This happened because Hitler went into an uncontrolled rage over the incident, damned the Geneva Convention rules, and ordered the Gestapo and ss to administer the policies, if not the actual management of the Luftwaffe camps.

Later that day, the men in the boxcars would experience their first taste of the new brutality that awaited them. "The goons came around and handcuffed everybody in pairs and we had no idea why; there was no way to escape with all the guards around. So, I was hooked to Russ and I think both of us sensed that things were going to get worse."

The train finally pulled out that evening when the other kriegies were loaded, and Slats remembers little of their all-night ride except that it was "miserable as hell standing up for another night. We did manage to help ourselves a bit when one guy found a loose board on the wall that they were able to break and give us a hole where we could relieve ourselves."

The next morning the train chugged into a station named Kiefheide (now Podborsko, Poland). When the doors were opened Slats, along with the estimated two thousand other kriegies, was looking forward to getting unshackled, and to the new camp where he could wash, get food, and lie down on a bed. But as soon as they left their boxcars and wandered up to the train station, two lines of guards from Stalag Luft IV in gray-blue uniforms formed on each side of them and marched them into the village of Gross Tychow (now Gmina Tychowo, Poland). There, a captain in a white uniform stood on a platform and began raging at them. Except for the German speakers none of them could understand what he was saying, but they all knew from his manner and motions that they were words of anger and hate. Then he was followed on the platform by a small officer whose shouts and rantings were even more vitriolic. A German speaker near Slats yelled to those near him that they were to start running on the dirt road ahead of them that ran through a woods and led to their new camp. At first, the men refused as the guards began yelling at them. But then a group of teenage Krieg marines (naval cadets) with rifles and bayonets moved in on them, hitting some with their rifle butts and jabbing others with the point of their bayonets. Also alongside them were guards with vicious, snarling dogs on leashes, and they were urged by their handlers to attack and bite stragglers. Soon the narrow road was filled with struggling men—many had injuries that prevented them from running—while being brutalized by rifle butts, bayonets, and savage dogs. In addition, there were machine guns in the woods along the road. By some accounts they were hidden because it was the hope of the commandant that, by forcing the men to run, many would try to escape into the woods, and this would be an excuse to murder many of them. Slats himself does not remember seeing or hearing about the machine guns that others have described. And, at this time, if he had known about Dante's *Inferno*, he would have known that he had just been thrust down into the fourth circle of hell.

# CHAPTER 12

## Stalag Luft IV

There have been several accounts written of the forced run to Stalag Luft IV, and most of them detail the horror. A future son of one of the kriegies has written about his father's back injury that caused an early death when he was in his fifties. He said that he would never talk about how he received his original injury, saying that it was something he was trying to wipe out of his memory. One day, as he was dying, the son asked again and all his father would say was, "A guy hit me in the back with a rifle butt." He knew, of course, that this occurred on the run to the prison camp.

We will never know the extent of the injuries suffered by those two thousand–plus men who had to navigate that narrow roadway. But we do have the testimony of one of the doctors who treated some of them, Capt. Henry J. Wynsen's. According to a military intelligence report now available online, Wynsen's deposition was given to the Judge Advocate General's Investigator on July 20, 1945—almost exactly a year after the event:

Captain Wynsen stated that on July 17, 18, 19, and August 5 and 6, 1944, he and Capt. Wilber McKee treated injured American and British soldiers, who had been bayoneted, clubbed, and bitten by dogs, while on route from the railroad station to Stalag Luft IV, a distance of approximately three kilometers [almost two miles]. Most of the injuries were bayonet wounds, which varied from a break in the skin to puncture wounds three inches deep. The usual site was the buttock; hit sites included the back, flanks, and even the neck. The number of wounds varied from one to as many as sixty. One American soldier suffered severe dog bites on the calves of both legs, necessitating months of treatment in bed. The first bayonet patient seen by Dr. Wynsen was in a hysterical condition with a puncture wound in the buttock. A medical tag was fastened to his shirt with a diagnosis of "sun stroke." For his "sun stroke" the man had been given tetanus antitoxin. This diagnosis was made by a German captain named Summers. . . . It was estimated that there were over one hundred American and British that were bayoneted during the course of these runs to the Stalag.

Unfortunately, this was only the beginning of the brutality campaign that was being launched in most of the Luftwaffe camps. When the kriegies arrived in the big yard of Laager A—there were four laagers (compounds), A, B, C, and D—they were forced to spend the rest of the day and probably (accounts vary) two more days with no food, and perhaps a little water. This apparently was intended on the part of the commandant, Oberst (Lt. Col.) Albert Bambach, to get the message across that this camp would in no way be like the one the kriegies had just come from. The commandant of Luft VI was a letter-of-the-law executor of the Geneva

Convention. Bambach, on the other hand, totally ignored the rights of prisoners written into that treaty. For example, T.Sgt. Frank Paulus had been the elected leader (man-of-confidence) in Luft VI—some accounts say that he received 80 percent of the votes—but this commandant ignored the kriegies who demanded that Paulus be given the leadership role here, instead appointing T.Sgt. Richard M. Chapman. The message: true Nazis do not believe in elections. (Eventually, because of the action of the men, Paulus was recognized as the leader.)

So, what did the kriegie new arrivals do in that big yard while they toughed out the German-engineered initiation to the Nazi world? The first thing that many remember was the disgusting behavior of the guards during the mandatory search of everyone's personal effects. Everything personal, like razors, soap, books, toiletries, watches, and rings, had to be thrown down in front of each kriegie. Then a guard would go through everything. Some would take whatever they wanted for themselves—things like watches and cigarette cases. But others, just to show off their authority, would take things like toiletry articles and highly revered family photos. Or they might tear a religious medal off a kriegie's neck. Undoubtedly, there were many angry expressions when such personal items were taken. Also, one can speculate that the more sadistic of the guards got great enjoyment from seeing such expressions. As for Slats, he said, "They didn't take anything like that from me because I had nothing."

And then the men did something else, and to appreciate their actions, the reader needs to understand how vastly different the growing-up years were for these kriegies, compared to how the baby boomers and modern young people have been raised. Boys who grew up on farms and the small towns of America, which was where most of these kriegies were raised, typically did two things when they finished their school year. First, they shed their shoes, and except perhaps for church or some other formal affair, they would stay barefoot until the sad, sad day when school started and they had to put them back on again. And yes, there was a period when the feet had to get "toughened." But, within a week or so, by deliberately walking on the roads paved with shale or crushed gravel, they then jumped and skidded on these kinds of surfaces just to show their peers how tough their feet had become. The second thing they did was peel off their shirts. Yes, there were a few "sissy" boys who did not want to do that, or whose parents objected. These unfortunate boys, even if their parents would let them, could not accompany the other boys to a favorite swimming "hole"—typically a pond, creek, or reservoir. Why? Because with their snow-white bodies, they (1) would be teased and ridiculed, and (2) they would suffer terrible sunburn from the mid-summer rays. In short, having tough feet and a deep suntan were the badges of honor. And while the high school students usually came around to the wearing of shoes in the summer, the deep upper-body suntan continued to be the respectable social badge up through early manhood.

So, again the question: What did these kriegies do when they got to Laager A yard and had to spend one or two days in the sun? They peeled their shirts off, and if they already had the beginning of a tan started in their earlier camp, they kept their shirts off during daylight hours for the entire time they waited. In Slats's words while describing the looks of the kriegies in the yard: "It looked like a nudist colony out there."

But Slats was not one of them, and it was not just because he grew up in a city environment. "When I was thirteen or fourteen, my mother went to visit a sister in Wadena, Minnesota, and she took me with her. They lived on a farm, and when we got there, a threshing crew was doing the preliminary work, which was to take the tied bundles that had been made with a binder and stand them up in small stacks, or shocks. What impressed me was that all of them, I think, were working without their shirts. Boy, I wanted to get right out there with them, so I peeled off my shirt and I started building shocks with the rest of them. What a terrible mistake.

"Actually, a horrible mistake. With the pale, freckled skin of a redhead, I got badly sunburned—I mean it was real bad. Oh, how I suffered that next day. I was really in pain. That taught me a lesson that I have obeyed up to this day."

For some reason that he cannot now remember, while out in the yard, he was selected by a guard and told to follow. What he does remember is the remorse he felt that his now very close friend, Russell Schlyer, was not ordered to go with him. But, dutifully, he followed and was taken to a room in one of the wooden dormitory-type buildings. When he entered, he discovered that he was the first one there, so he immediately selected the top bunk at the end of a row of eight double-deckers. Later, he was to see Russell one or two times in the yard of Laager D, but they were never to be together after that.

His first chore, and for the fifteen others who came into the room, was to trek out to the straw stack. There they were given big sacks and told to fill them with the straw—that these would be their mattresses. He remembers stuffing as much as he could in his sack, realizing that it was brittle and would soon break into finer pieces and provide less cushioning. But, when he got back to the room, someone had placed five bed slats on each bed. "That was nothing. I mean, how are you going to arrange just five slats so you can lie on them without part of you going through the big cracks? And, yes, because of my nickname, I was constantly reminded that slats are what the tunnel builders use to shore up the walls to keep them from falling in—that's why they only gave us five of them—we couldn't sleep at night if even one was missing. But what a pain."

Next, this twenty-year-old young man who eighteen months earlier thought of himself as an inferior person, got a surprise. After they returned from the straw pile, they were informed by a representative from the camp leader that each room was to elect a room chief, whose main chores were to supervise the behavior of the men, enforce cleanliness in the room, and be in charge of security. Almost before Slats could even think about it, the other fifteen unanimously agreed that he should have the job. He admits that this was a surprise, but that he immediately felt "up to the responsibility" and agreed to take it on. Looking back, he now says, deprecatingly, "Probably nobody else in there wanted that kind of responsibility laid on them and they picked me because I hadn't said anything."

His first big challenge as room chief came just a few days later. The barracks chief (there were ten rooms in Barracks 9, where he lived) came to him one day with a problem. "He explained to me that there was a young man in one of the other rooms that was worrying everybody. He said that this guy goes outside and stands just inside the warning wire just looking at it, and that whenever anybody tries to talk to him, he won't say a word or he'll tell the guy to leave him alone. And, worst of all, he won't even tell anybody his name. He just clams up. And this barracks chief—I can't remember his name—then asks me if I would try to talk to him because he was afraid this guy was thinking of doing something drastic.

"Well, I agreed to do it, figuring that something had happened upstairs [in the sky] that he was feeling bad about or guilty about. After getting a description of the guy—he was thought to be no older than nineteen and I was told that he was smaller than me—I noticed a guy I thought might be him standing in the hall just looking down at the floor. I went up to him and tried to be friendly. I told him that some of the guys around him were worried about him and that we all wanted to help him. He kept looking at the floor while I talked. But I went on and explained that, if he was feeling guilty about doing something while on a mission, that he was probably making too big a deal out of it. When he didn't react, I remember saying, 'Hey, look, we're in a war, we were fighting for our lives up there, and any of us could have made a mistake—so if you did make some kind of mistake, we all just have to put it behind us and get on with our lives.'

"I don't think a thing I said registered with him; I think that whatever he had done just took over his whole mind. And it wasn't much after that I was in my room and heard machine-gun fire just outside. I ran out and it was him, lying on the ground just outside the wire. The whole laager came out and watched as the guards came and carried him away. That was sure a downer for us, but I've thought about what I said to him many times and, each time, I decided that I would have said exactly the same things to him if I had to do it over again."

It was not long before Slats began to establish a routine to defy the boredom. First on his list of priorities was to continue the running routine he had started in the almost two-month stay in Luft VI. Although his knee was much better and he no longer had a significant limp, he sensed that the hard physical pounding it would take while running would cause it to continually improve. So after morning roll call, alone now, he would run around the yard. After several more weeks of running, the pain was barely noticeable and he could feel that he also had more strength. He probably hadn't heard of "atrophy," but his thigh muscles had to have atrophied during the two and a half months or so that they were inactive. His running in Luft VI, and later in Luft IV, had to have caused the regeneration of a lot of that lost muscle tissue.

What else? He continued to play poker, and after about a month, when they received their first Red Cross parcels with their five small packs of cigarettes, he began winning so many cigarettes that there was no way he could use them up in trading. And, even though he would have willingly given some of them to the heavy smokers in his room, that would have been equivalent to a serious crime. Cigarettes were the camp money and for that money to retain its value, a kriegie who did anything to undercut its value would be in big trouble with the other inmates. So what do you do if you have several hundred cigarettes and cannot get rid of them? Slats solved that problem by the one option open to him: he started smoking. "And, boy, was that pure hell for a while. I got sick and I got dizzy, and at times I thought I was going to pass out. And, eventually, I got used to it, then got hooked like all the other smokers. But I still continued to win more than I smoked, so I always had trading material."

He also learned a new game while in Luft IV, the card game called bridge. Before the days when television came along and almost destroyed the evening social interactions in towns and cities, many adults belonged to bridge clubs where, typically, four or five "tables" would gather once a week at some member's home, play bridge for an hour or so, adjourn for refreshments, then reconvene for another hour. And these were anything but fun-and-laughter parties; bridge was a deadly serious game. Players talked in hushed voices, and even after a hand was finished, there was little conversation because it could disturb the concentration of others. Of course, Slats did not grow up with bridge-playing parents, so he knew absolutely nothing about the game. But in his room was an older kriegie named Jim McKenzie, who was a very skilled player and who needed a partner in order to join a game. It was probably his observation of Slats's skill at the poker table that made him think he could quickly teach Slats this much more complicated game. For whatever reason, he extended the offer, Slats accepted, and true to McKenzie's probable expectations, Slats learned quickly under his tutelage and was soon a skilled player. When asked about his bridge partner's personality, Slats hesitated, then said, "Jim had a strange idea about exercise. He said that he didn't want to do any of it because he didn't want to use up any of his energy. I heard him say several times, 'I want to save and store up all the energy I can because I may need it sometime.' That may have been just his way of needling me about my running, but, later, this lack of exercise could really have been a problem for him."

The days passed slowly, but they did pass. And, with the brain's need for stimulation driving the kriegies' behavior, few suffered the Beetle Bailey syndrome. If it was not poker or bridge, it was softball or boxing or a musical instrument or impromptu classes conducted by those with special knowledge or skills. Then there was reading, one of the most potent of all brain-stimulating exercises. And while Slats insists that he knew nothing of a library in Luft IV, he somehow managed to acquire enough books that he spent a part of every day engrossed in a story.

However, far and away the most stimulating and exciting experiences for all the kriegies were the news stories that reached them via their secret radio and spread barracks to barracks by news reporting specialists. A big story happened the second day after their arrival: on July 20 there had been an unsuccessful assassination attempt made on Hitler inside his Polish command bunker. And, yes, there were to be repercussions that would ultimately affect all of them, but that did not stop the cheering in their hearts and the wishful *if only it could have been successful* thoughts that had to have crossed their minds.

Then there were the daily suspense stories of Allied movements in France. There was the breakout at St. Lo that allowed the armies to escape the deadly hedgerows in the Normandy peninsula. Then it was the bigger breakout through the Falaise Gap that resulted in the capture of a German army and enabled General Patton's mechanized Third Army to lunge toward Paris. And then on the August 25 BBC broadcast there came the great news that Paris was free and mostly undamaged. Slats, of course, does not remember specific dates, but the thrill of such great news still rings in his memory.

Also, the rumor was still going around about the U.S. government's deal with the Soviets to pay a prize for each prisoner they freed. In Slats's mind it was definitely a fifty-dollar prize and he insists that he, personally, really believed that liberation would come from the Soviet sector. Of course, he was in what is now Poland and with Warsaw threatened, it was logical to assume that liberators would be coming from that direction.

So the weeks went by and summer became autumn. And that brought heavy overcasts, rain, and weather that got damper and colder. Gone were the bare backs and the outdoor buddy bathing—baths where buddies like Slats and McKenzie took turns soaping, sudsing, and rinsing each other. And always the questions: What is taking those damn Soviets so long to get here? What happened to Patton and why isn't he charging through Germany like he did in France? As of October 5 and 6, according to an official count by a visiting Red Cross official there were 7,089 Americans, in addition to 886 Brits, 147 Canadians, 37 Australians, 22 New Zealanders, 8 South Africans, 1 Norwegian, 2 Frenchmen, 58 Poles, and 5 Czechs in Stalag Luft IV, practically all of them waiting in suspense to hear what the next BBC news bulletin reported.

## CHAPTER 13

## Goons, Ferrets, and Some Good Guy Stories

The comic strip artist and writer Milton Caniff introduced his readers to a lot of interesting characters while he was creating *Terry and the Pirates* back in the '30s and '40s. One of them was Big Stoop, a nine-foot-tall Mongol who was a pretty good guy. At Stalag Luft IV a guard by the name of Hans Schmidt was not that tall, but the kriegies who had to deal with him called him Big Stoop and insisted that he was anywhere from six-foot-eight to seven feet tall, with a powerful build and extraordinarily large hands. And perhaps the reader, after reading stories about some of his actions, can think of a more appropriate name to describe this goon.

The first story was related by Slats: "I was standing in the yard one day talking to some kriegie friends when Big Stoop walked up to them and addressed Abe Homar, who was standing beside me. He told Abe to state his name and when Abe answered, he only got out the word 'Abraham' when Big Stoop swats him with one of those big ham hands and Abe goes down like a ton of bricks. Stoop then goes on his way and Abe gets up and says, 'I sure wish I had a name like Slayton.'" The problem was Stoop hated Jews.

The following is an excerpt from testimony given by Dr. Leslie Caplan, one of the camp doctors, before the War Crimes Office investigating the mistreatment of American prisoners at Stalag Luft IV:

Q. For what reason was "Big Stoop" disliked?

A. He beat up on many of our men. He would cuff the men on the ears with an open hand sideway movement. This would cause pressure on the eardrums, which sometimes punctured them.

Q. Could you give any specific incidents of such mistreatment by "Big Stoop"?

A. Yes, I treated some of the men whose eardrums had been ruptured by the cuffings administered by "Big Stoop."

Next is a story related by S.Sgt. Don Kirby that shows the extreme anger of those who had been brutalized by Big Stoop:

Now, we had a "Big Stoop" with us and he was something else. He was a big goon who was maybe seven feet tall, looked like Primo Carnera [giant Italian world heavyweight boxing champion], and was all mean. He had hurt my friend Tinker and one time we came close to a confrontation. One of Stoop's favorite things was to grab a hold of your hand, and play like he was just joking . . . then twist up your thumb or something. One time on Christmas, when we had just what little stuff we could put together all set out, he walked in our barracks and turned over the whole dinner table. Some guy had a couple of little cans of jam and some special food we'd been saving. . . . There's times in your life when you just say:

Now, I'm not going along with this anymore. . . . I'm not putting up with this shit anymore! We were in the barracks and I was lying up on my bunk . . . just simmering about something. Tinker was below me and the word had just spread: Big Stoop is coming! I was on my back with my forearm on my face and one arm dangling over the side of the bunk. Tink said to me, "Kirby, get your hand up or Stoop will grab it." I don't know what was in me that day, but I felt ornery. I said to myself, "If he does grab it, I'm gonna hit the S.O.B. with everything in this place." There was no doubt in my mind that I was going to do it. Tinker whispered: "Come on, get it up." But I let that thing hang down there. Now here comes that goon. He's sitting around with a couple of kriegies over there and the time is just passing. I felt his glance sweep over toward me a couple of times, but I just lay there. Whether he just didn't care . . . at any rate, he just walked on by. But, if he'd made a move on me, so help me God, I would have done him in. Of course, I'd have gotten shot.

Now, one more story told by S.Sgt. Stratton Beesley regarding Big Stoop's actions after the kriegies first arrived at Luft IV and when the guards were searching and examining their personal possessions: "I did see Big Stoop confiscate pictures from companions of mine and rub them on his private parts while grinning like an ape. I learned later that these were pictures of wives and girlfriends of the POWs."

Big Stoop had to have been one of the most sadistic of the goons in Luft IV, but there were others with names like Green Hornet and Squarehead and Cowboy and Smiley and a one-eyed guard that somehow got the name of Hollywood. But who were these goons, and with Germany struggling to get enough men in the front lines on two war fronts, how did they luck out with such safe and easy duty?

Some of them were old—too old to withstand the rigors of frontline combat. In his postwar testimony Dr. Caplan estimated Big Stoop's age as "fifty," and Slats said, if he had to guess, some of them were between fifty-five and sixty-five.

Many of the others had wounds that physically disabled them; for example, Captain Weinart, the officer in charge of Laager C, was a former prisoner captured by the Americans in North Africa and repatriated because of a debilitating arm wound.

And then there was another category that is best revealed in a story told by T.Sgt. Carter Lunsford, who was Frank Paulus's deputy:

Some of the German noncommissioned officers at the camp came from families that were well connected politically and were there to keep out of the conflict. Two or three of them spoke excellent English and they came to Frank [Paulus—now recognized as camp leader]. They realized the war was going against them and that the better they handled us, the better the results they would get at the end. [They said,] "Look, we feel that the commandant is being too strict with you. What we would like to do is prove to him that you can get a man out any time you want to; and all this tight security is a waste. It's not preventing any escapes at all. We'll help you do that [prove that you do not want to escape]. Do you have anyone who can speak German?" Of course, Bill Krebs did! They brought in two German Luftwaffe uniforms with a pass all prepared. The colonel knew in advance that we were going to try and get a man out. He was lined up outside his headquarters with his staff, waiting to see if we could do it. He had agreed that if we succeeded, he would relax these midnight raids. To my mind it was a brave thing for Bill Krebs to attempt. It's quite possible that they could have shot him.

*Goons, Ferrets, and Stories*

We were lined up for evening roll call, and he slipped away to put on the Luftwaffe uniform with the pass. After the count, he went out of the compound and through the gates of the Vorlager with the other guards. As he went out, we could see him chatting with his new buddies. They let him pass outside of the Vorlager and no one questioned him whatsoever. There's this colonel with all his staff just waiting to nab us in our escape attempt. Bill gave him the Heil Hitler salute and continued walking about a dozen paces before he turned on his heels and came back. Standing in front of Bombach, he gave a snappy salute and said: "William Krebs, United States Air Corps!" Isn't that something!

When he got back into the compound, we asked him, "Bill, what did you say to those guards?" He said, "Oh, well . . . this day's over! I'm going now to get a cup of coffee and a bit of sausage!"

Despite the brutality at this level of hell, there were occasions when Slats and the other kriegies had something to cheer about. One such occasion was when one of the goons who had climbed a power pole accidentally touched two wires and the current shot through his body. When this happened, everybody rushed out and watched as he laid back in his climbing belt, his hair standing straight out and his face changing color. Slats was one of the thousands "cheering and yelling for the kraut to fall and get it done with. But then some of the other guards started firing over us and we ran like hell for cover. I know I hid behind our barracks and peeked out occasionally. He finally did fall and they carried him away."

More cheering occurred while they were outside watching three ME-109s do a low flyover their camp. This brought all the men out, including Slats, who then watched as the three fighters made another low pass. After that, they turned around and came back for another pass; however, the top fighter was now flying upside down. Obviously, they were showing off for the kriegies; however, the one flying upside down suddenly nosed down through his mates and dove into the ground, exploding when it hit. The thousands of cheering kriegies got away with this display—at least, Slats cannot remember any adverse actions from the guards.

However, the goons also got an opportunity to cheer a kriegie misfortune. Slats tells that story: "It was one evening when it was raining like hell and lightning was all over the place—I mean the thunder was shaking the walls. I had been lying in my bunk—we couldn't read at night because the only light we had was candles—and I had to go take a leak. I remember, I was doing it against the masonry wall at the end of the barracks when a big bolt of lightning came down and it was so close, it scared me to death. I just stood there and shivered. I thought it had hit the barracks, but then I found out that it had hit just twenty or thirty feet away—there were four guys in Laager B, British guys playing cards in a little hut, and that lightning bolt killed all four of them. I later found out that they were some of the first ones in Luft IV—they had come in before we did. Talk about being scared—I was shaking I was so scared. I could actually feel a little bit of that bolt of lightning."

That incident was a downer for the whole camp and some of the kriegies have commented about how some of the goons eased up on them for the next few days. But there is another story Slats remembers, which happened a little after this tragedy, that raised their spirits a bit. "We had this character in our barracks and he was always doing crazy things. One day at roll call—he was in the front row—the barracks commander, Major Gruber, a stiff Prussian, was up in front of us and he clicked his heels, gives the Nazi salute, and yells the

'Heil Hitler' number. Right after that, this guy clicks his heels, gives the Nazi salute, and yells, 'Hail to the führer, the fewer the better!' Gruber comes right back, gives the salute, and repeats what this guy said. Boy, did we have trouble keeping from laughing."

Slats remembers another story, this one about another kind of bad guy in the camp: "We had several ferrets that roamed around the camp—these were guys who were working for the Germans to get information from us. An example was a guy who came into our room one day and in perfect American English began visiting with us. We were all intrigued because this guy talked just like us and so we started asking him questions. He said he grew up in Michigan—Saginaw, I think—and went on to say that after the war, he was really looking forward to getting back there. Boy, this one guy in the room really let him have it. He said, 'You dirty, rotten son-of-a-bitch, I'm from Saginaw and if I ever see you when I get home, I'll kill you.' That didn't faze this guy a bit. He said, 'I'm not a bit worried about you because, when you get home, you'll be thinking about getting on with your life and you won't even remember who I am.' How's that for guts? I've always wished I knew more about that story—how he got into the ferret business and what happened to him."

So, besides the goons, the Germans had ferrets around the camp and their job was to go into the rooms, start friendly conversations, and hope that the kriegies would accidentally tell him something that would be useful to the camp administrators. Slats thinks there were several of them that would wander from one laager to the next, always trying to "buddy up" with some of the guys. Also, some were reportedly walking around in kriegie-type clothing so they would not be recognized. Slats remembers getting warnings about some of them and, because as room chief he was in charge of security, it was his duty when he detected them coming toward their room to yell "forty-four" as a warning for what was going to happen.

There were also some guards who were good guys, and S.Sgt. James Ross tells about two of them:

We also had two guards that would get together and come to our barracks. Asche was the name of one of them and he was a teacher, as was Snyder, the other. One of our guys was interested in birds and we had a nature book. These two guards were interested . . . so they would come in to chat with us and look at our books. The next thing we knew an hour would go by . . . [later] if Asche came in . . . and there were only two or three of us, he would sit down and tell us about his family. He had two sisters and his folks were meat cutters (butchers). He told us where he went to grade school and high school and on to Heidelberg University. His family had a car and was considered middle class. He'd tell us about Germany and how things were before Hitler. It was the middle class that was hurt the most in Germany. Listening to Asche and some of the other decent guards is why when people ask me if I hated the Germans, I always said, "No, I hated the Nazis."

In Stalag Luft IV there was something else that all of them hated: the cold and the damp air that was beginning to descend upon the camp.

## CHAPTER 14

## Winter Descends

Most depictions of an inferno emphasize that it is an environment of fire and heat. However, another expression has also been around for a while: *It's cold as hell out there!* And that is the way it was becoming in level four of Slats Slayton's and the other kriegies' inferno.

But what depressed the kriegies in Stalag Luft IV more than the cold and the other miseries, like inadequate and maggot-infested food, brutal goons, and lack of hot water for bathing, were questions like these: What the hell was Ike thinking letting that ego maniac, Montgomery, get men slaughtered in Operation Market Garden? And: Where the hell is Patton—he made it to Paris in just a few days and he should be on his way to Berlin right now—is Ike holding him back to make the English look good? And: Why did those damn Russians back off and not take Warsaw immediately?

For weeks, especially after the rapid liberation of Paris, the optimists in the camp were betting their precious little money cylinders (some were now complaining that after several transactions half the tobacco had fallen out of them) that the Germans would be defeated by Christmas and they would celebrate that holiday by being free again. And these hopes even spread to some of the realists like Slats, who admits that he reluctantly caught some of that fever. However, as October passed into November, and as the weather began to deteriorate, so did the news they were getting from the BBC. The Allies in the west were bogging down "against fierce German resistance at their borders"—news that compounded the cold and gloom of the deepening late autumn weather.

Conditions in the barracks got harsher. Eight men had been added to Slats's room, men who had no beds and who had to sleep on the floor. And the rooms were not really shelters from the cold, because the allotment of coke for their tiny stoves was totally inadequate. However, thanks to one of the new men in the room, Robert Arthur from Berlin, New Jersey, that condition started to improve. Arthur seemed to have a special talent for foraging, and he started becoming more and more proficient in pilfering coke. The good news was that as his skills increased, so did the average daytime temperatures of their room. Slats does not remember if Arthur was ever officially toasted with some of the kickapoo juice the kriegies were now making from the precious raisins they hoarded from the few Red Cross parcels they received, but he does remember that, in a room ceremony, he was officially christened with the name of Coke collector.

The crowding in the room and the confining conditions brought more problems for Slats, especially with his responsibility to keep the room neat and clean. "I had two guys, both from Brooklyn," he says, "that were about as messy as two guys could get. I don't want to use their names because it might embarrass their kids or grandkids, but talk about slovenly. They had dirt around their bed, stuff scattered everywhere—it just got so bad that I had to do something about it. So, one evening, in front of the others, I told them that I was kicking them out of the room, that they had to sleep out in the hall. Oh, they hated me, as you can imagine, but they also knew I had the support of the rest of the guys so they couldn't do anything about it. So they slept out in the hall, and the next day, one of them came back in the room and said, 'That's a bunch of BS sleeping out in that hall,' and began to clean up the dirt and pick up their crap. The other one didn't make a move to help him, but because the area was clean again, I let them both come back. But, you had to do that. If the goons had come in and seen that mess, they would probably have torn up the whole room."

Slats thinks it was late October or early November when two good things happened to him. First, one day while he was passing out the mail to the twenty-three others in his room—mail chief had been added to his duty of room chief—he looked down at the name on one of the envelopes and it was his own name. Quickly, he tossed the letter on his bed, but then he found another, and another, and another—seven letters total. "They were all from my mother and they had finally caught up with me, the first since I'd been a POW. There're really no words to describe your feelings when something like that happens. I know I didn't do anything else the rest of that day; I just laid in my bunk and read and reread them."

The second good thing that happened to him was that he finally got a close friend to replace Russell Schlyer, who had been forced to go to Laager D. It all started when, one day, they were all pretty well confined to their room because of bad weather, and Slats happened to notice one of the new men sitting on the floor, but obviously uncomfortable because of the cramped space he was in. Slats, who was sitting on his top bunk, motioned for the guy to join him on his bunk. He did and they started talking, found they had a lot in common, and soon the two of them were running and exercising in the yard together. "His name was Irwin J. Piere and he was from Eau Claire, Wisconsin, and for some reason he said that he had always been called Sam." Many years later, Slats was reminded by his now-old friend that he had performed an act of incredible generosity when he invited Sam to join him on the mattress that he had just plumped and made comfortable—that by inviting another man to sit on it anytime he wanted, he was accelerating the damage to the straw that was cushioning him from the hard bed slats.

The weather continued to deteriorate and even Slats and his friend, Sam, began to back off a bit on their outdoor exercising. And, besides the ever gloomy war news that the carriers were bringing to the rooms, word also began to spread that their duty to always be looking for ways of escaping from their confinement had been officially waived. Slats cannot remember for sure when he heard that and admits that it could have been earlier, but it was almost a moot point with all of them since, after the dramatic "Krebs escape," it was obvious that it would be a waste of time to try tunneling or any other means of escaping. They all knew that it would be a lot better to sit and wait it out, even though there were constant reminders from the pessimists among them that the Gestapo, on Hitler's orders, could come in and gun them down any day.

November moved slowly by and Slats cannot remember anything about Thanksgiving except that it was probably just another day of bad or little food and miserable conditions. Then it was December, and reports said U.S. troops were moving toward the Rhine River, a potentially major obstacle that was a long way from Berlin, where the fanatical Hitler was still screaming at his commanders to never retreat and to fight to the last man. Then came a day that

*Winter Descends*

every kriegie in Germany will remember. It was December 16, and before dawn that morning the four American divisions in the Ardennes Forest, about thirty-five miles west of the Rhine, were treated to a massive hour-and-a-half-long artillery bombardment along a forty-five-mile front. That was followed by an attack by twenty-four Panzer and army divisions that quickly sliced through that front, destroyed one of the American divisions, and resulted in the capture of about six thousand Americans. The other three divisions hurriedly retreated, became disorganized, and practically all communication with the units by Gen. Omar Bradley, who was in charge of that sector of the front, was either confused or lost. Of course, the kriegies, through their BBC link, could not have known specific details, but they did know that it was a major German counterattack that would, to some degree, definitely prolong the war.

Slats clearly remembers how the morale tanked after they learned about this new German offensive. Its degree of success would not have been reported by the BBC—bad news was always censored for home front morale purposes, but the kriegies not only could imagine the worst, but undoubtedly had observed enough buoyant expressions on the faces of their goons to increase its negative impact.

And there was an immediate effect, at least in Laager A. Someone started spreading the word: if we're going to be stuck in this place past Christmas, why waste two precious cigarettes for a haircut, why don't we just shave our heads? Somehow, this message became some kind of antidote to the dismal war news, and soon kriegies in Laager A—Slats is not sure about the other three laagers—were lining up by the hundreds, grinning and laughing, for the camp barbers to convert them to skinheads. When asked why he did it, especially as the bitter winter weather had descended upon them, Slats could only say, lamely, "I can't remember any logical reason . . . we were cooped up like chickens or cattle and I guess it was just a way to tell the goons that we still had some control over our lives—that they couldn't control everything we did. And we were young and young people do some stupid things, you know."

Now Christmas was coming and every kriegie had accepted the fact that liberation was weeks, if not months, away. Also, the news coming from the BBC was anything but good, and while they probably did not hear the details of the German successes, the lack of details, and probably the smug expressions of their goons, further darkened their spirits. And what were the chances that this latest German thrust could in any way be successful? Probably this was discussed at length. And surely some of the analytical thinkers had come up with the ideal and practical solution to this latest offensive: Why not let the bastards keep going—just keep gasoline away from them—and those panzers will eventually be stranded and they can then be wiped out. Actually, it was reported after the war that this is exactly what General Patton argued with Eisenhower. "Hell, let them go on to Paris, they'll just bog down, and that will be twenty-four less divisions we'll have to fight," he is reported to have said.

Then, two days before Christmas, they may have heard the first good news coming from the Ardennes. The skies had cleared—skies that had kept Allied aircraft from attacking the invaders. Soon beleaguered troops at strategic cities like Bastogne were receiving needed supplies from air drops, and to the German commanders who had been brought from the Soviet front, the massive fighter attacks on their tanks and troops was a war experience that was virtually new. The next day, on December 24, the two panzer divisions reached their maximum thrust of about sixty miles. Between the air attacks and the more mundane fact that their tanks had run out of gas, the men of those two divisions had no choice but to abandon their equipment and start retreating on foot. This was particularly humiliating to one of General Von Rundstedt's key leaders, ss Gen. Joachim Peiper, who barely escaped being captured while hiking back through the deep snow. Another key factor in the German debacle was the arrival of a division from Patton's Third Army in Bastogne just after Christmas, an event that the kriegies undoubtedly heard on the BBC because Patton was such a favorite with the news media.

How did this German offensive affect the length of the war and the kriegies' ultimate liberation? Sir Arthur Tedder, Eisenhower's deputy supreme commander, wrote on December 22, "The fact that the Hun has stuck his neck out is, from the point of view of shortening the whole business, the best thing that could happen. It may make months of difference."

Slats says they were keenly tuned to the war news, but that practical matters dominated the kriegies' thoughts when the big holiday arrived. Luckily, two factors, one human and the other natural, made Christmas Eve a memorable event in their lives. Here is Slats's own account, written many years later:

I can still recall as though it were yesterday the events of the evening of December 24, 1944. . . . We, as prisoners of war, had asked permission of our German Kommandant to be allowed out of our barracks on that Christmas evening for a short period of time. Permission granted, seventy-five hundred American prisoners in four separate compounds walked around their fenced areas. The harsh setting of barbed wire and armed sentry posts were being softened by huge star-like snowflakes, which lazily drifted groundward. Suddenly, over the soft shuffle of feet, rising softly at first, and then swelling as all joined in, the sound of seventy-five hundred male voices were raised in song and the strains of "White Christmas" filled the air. It was awesome, beautiful, and a most unforgettable moment. Christmas carols were sung for the entire hour with German guards listening intently and those nearby even commenting. Our spirits were lifted tremendously by this one hour. Still under the enchantment of Christmas Eve, Christmas Day followed with another pleasant surprise to add to this most memorable Christmas. The surprise was an American Red Cross Christmas food parcel with turkey and plum pudding for each and every one. You cannot imagine how tasty it was. We had expected so little and had received so much. Most of us ended that great day by giving thanks to the Lord for his bounty, [and] I was so moved by that day that I still find it difficult to speak of it. Such was my most memorable Christmas.

Despite the bitter news that meant liberation was definitely sometime in an indefinite future, the seventy-five hundred kriegies, embedded in a pine forest 659 miles of road from the now-relieved American forces in Bastogne, Belgium, continued to play poker and bridge and read books and make their cigarette bets on whether it would be their distant buddies on the Western Front, or the Soviets, now in their winter offensive and much closer, that would eventually free them from this miserable camp.

## CHAPTER 15

## Descent into the Fifth Circle

January brought bitter cold to much of Europe—accounts conflict on whether this was Europe's coldest winter in forty years or the coldest winter in recorded European history. However, despite the misery, Slats Slayton insists that he continued to brave the elements and exercised by running or walking periodically in the Laager A yard. He also remembers the ongoing bridge games that he and Jim McKenzie continued to win and the extra cigarettes that he now traded almost exclusively for books from other kriegies. According to the "Kriegie Book" that he managed to preserve, the last four of the forty-six titles penned in by Pop Brown—his older buddy who had come with him from Luft VI—were probably read in January or early February. The names of those last four books? *Botany Bay*, the story of the English prisoners who first settled in Australia; then *Chad Hanna*, a great novel about circus life in the 1830s; then *Payment Deferred*, a book from in C. S. Forester's Horatio Hornblower series; and finally *Box Office*, a book of famous short stories that had been used as themes for outstanding movies.

Several mornings during these winter months, Slats would wake up and hear from the others in the room that bombs had been heard exploding south of them. "I couldn't have heard them," said Slats, "because I was such a sound sleeper." They never knew for certain where the bombs were falling, but they did know the German city of Stettin was in that direction and assumed that night bombers from England were hitting it.

Then, in late January, two significant things happened. First, they heard the sounds of artillery east of them—some have said they also saw lights from the exploding shells—that they assumed were the Soviets now nearing their area. Of course, there was speculation, even hope, that this would be a liberating force.

The second thing that happened dashed all their hopes of liberation. On January 25 or 26—perhaps on both days—about twenty-five hundred kriegies marched down to the train station and were put in boxcars for transportation to another camp. Soon after that, the rumor mill was buzzing with information that many, perhaps most of those who were taken away, were the sick and the injured and those deemed too frail to evacuate west on foot. "We're next, we're next," went the message, always spoken with remorse because most of them had been evacuated from Stalag Luft VI because of the approaching Soviets, and the same thing now seemed a certainty.

So, despite no official statement from the commander that they were going to evacuate, many of the kriegies began serious preparations. Some accounts of those days say that the rooms were like sewing factories, where kriegies took a spare shirt, sewed the bottom shut, then sewed the ends of the sleeves in such a way that the shirt could become a backpack, the sleeves serving as the straps. There were other

*Descent into the Fifth Circle*

individual refinements to the basic design, although Slats does not remember anyone in his room making such a home-made pack. As to his preparations, "I had just three posses-sions that I really cared about, my Bible, hymn book, and kriegie notebook. We had two blankets, a thin green Ger-man blanket and a thick GI wool one. I tore off a strip of the German blanket and used it to wrap my three books; then I took another strip, tied it around the package, and made a carrying handle. Also, thinking about walking in the cold, I didn't have any headgear like many of the others, so I used the rest of that thin blanket and figured out a way to wrap it so it would be a combination cap and scarf."

Then on Monday, February 5, the whole camp received two announcements. The first came in the morning, and it was word to the effect that Stalag Luft IV would not be evac-uated. Fortunately, few of the kriegies really believed that and they continued their preparation. Then, in the after-noon, came the second announcement, which confirmed their expectations: Stalag Luft IV would be evacuated start-ing the following morning. Slats and several others also think they were told that they were only going to have to walk for three days.

The next morning an estimated six thousand kriegies walked out of the camp in three groups, A, B, and C. Slats somehow got into the A group, and as they filed out, they went by a warehouse where they were allowed to take as many Red Cross food parcels as they felt they could carry. Then, on the first mile or two, as those trying to carry two or three of them realized the burden they had, many started throwing things away—things that they felt they would not need in the three days they were going to walk. Most threw away their second roll of toilet paper, and many, not realiz-ing that their bars of Ivory soap would become powerful trading merchandise with German women they would meet on their trek, threw one or both of those bars away. Slats had only taken one parcel, and he elected to keep everything, a fortuitous decision, as it turned out.

At first, they marched five abreast, always on narrow, unpaved roads, and in anything but a direct route. Soon, they learned that the guards escorting them along the sides of the column were, when possible, steering them clear of the many villages that lay along their route.

At the end of the day, after walking an estimated twelve to fifteen miles, Slats's group was broken up into groups of two to three hundred and directed to a farmer's barn. There, probably after receiving a chunk of black bread and a boiled potato or kohlrabi—German turnip—prepared in one of the big boilers that seemed to be present on every farm, the men pooled their blankets and tried to make beds on straw scattered over the barn floor. Most of the men were deeply chilled by this time and many removed their shoes and socks and examined their sore and blistered feet. Slats never had either of those problems. He had managed to get one of the long, heavy GI overcoats that the Red Cross had brought to the camp, and the fact that it was too big for him was a bonus; it extended well below his knees and the too-long sleeves helped protect his hands. As for his feet, all of that running the last eight months had toughened them with callouses, so they were not even a bit sore.

When they woke up the next morning, some of them felt something crawling on their body and began scratching or swatting their chest, back, or neck, while swearing loudly about the dirty little bastards that had crawled under their clothes during the night. Most of the country boys assumed they were lice for, during their growing-up years, they had either experienced the feel of them personally or, while in

*Descent into the Fifth Circle*

class in their one-room or small-town schools, observed their teacher, who regularly walked around the room, stopping now and then, and while a known louse-infested student continued to read or work on an assignment, she parted strands of the student's hair, picked off the lice, and crushed them between her thumbnails.

When the kriegies left the barn, they stood for roll call, then headed down the road again. As the first hour led into the second hour and then into the third hour, with only occasional short rest breaks, Slats must have heard many of those around him encouraging their lagging buddies with expressions like, "Just keep 'em moving, old buddy; we've only got to get through today and tomorrow." And what the reader must realize is that perhaps half or more of these young men had never walked more than five miles in any day of their life. Also, many of them, especially during the past three months while the weather was so cold and rainy, had been lying around on their bunks or just sitting and reading or playing cards, and were in terrible physical condition. So, despite the efforts of the guards to keep all of them walking at a strong pace, straggling became inevitable, and the original closely formed columns eventually stretched out for many miles.

Little of this affected Slats, and while they had been instructed at the beginning of the march to establish groups of three or four to share food and to make communal beds at night, he did not particularly care for the three others who had formed into his "combine." "One kid they called 'Lucky' was a bit of a smartass, and he was always wanting this and not wanting that, and the other two were not what I'd call 'my type.' So, especially when they started to straggle, I just went on and you can say that it was a bit like it was in the tail of the B-17—I began to appreciate the solitude and the feeling of independence."

The lack of drinking water was Slats's first significant problem. "You could definitely call me a 'water drinker,' and while we were walking, a truck might come by and throw us a loaf of bread to split, but seldom did they bring water. So, because there was snow off to the side of the roads we walked on, we started reaching down and grabbing handfuls to eat. Yeah, we instinctively knew that there were probably germs in it, but thirst is a powerful force—if you don't get water, your body starts crying for it."

That night the guards again broke them into groups of two or three hundred and escorted each group into a farmer's barn. And since Slats had broken away from his combine, he thinks it may have been this second night he found a place on the floor and began sharing his blanket with whoever happened to be bedding down next to him. And he has absolutely no idea what villages they passed nor how far they walked. But, according to an estimate based on another kriegie's sketchy notes recorded on this march—he never revealed how he was able to arrive at these numbers, especially when they were constantly making detours—they may have walked between twelve and sixteen miles that day.

Their third and "final" day was another long walk that led them to another barn in the bleak Pomeranian countryside. Probably not many gripes and negative comments were heard when it became obvious that the three-day march was a cruel German hoax—"quit your bitching" was a universal GI refrain when conditions grew worse. In other words, to the GI, tolerating misery was bad enough without being constantly reminded by others, which only made it harder to bear. And Slats's feeling when he learned that three days of marching did not lead them to the relative comfort of another Stalag Luft? "I think maybe I was a little better mentally prepared for this disappointment than some of the others. It was not much different than being trapped in the hold of that ship or standing for hours in a hot, crowded boxcar. You just tell yourself that you have absolutely no alternative; that no matter how bad or miserable you are, you just have to keep going and get through it."

However, if he was inclined to gripe, he now had something new that might have justified some bitching . . . because he also had the dirty little gray bastards crawling over his skin. "You could feel them on your neck and under your arms and down in your crotch—they always went for the warm places on your body," he said, remembering his first experience with lice. You just had to put up with them—it was way too cold to take off your clothes when you got to a barn—at night you just had to close your eyes, cover up as much as you could, and forget about them. Then, in the morning, when you're wide awake, you can really feel them, and, of course, during the night I'd probably pick up another bunch—that's probably why they bothered you most right after you woke up." The next morning it was "fall out" and stand for roll call, then perhaps a chunk of black bread, sometimes also a klim can of watery soup, and then down the road again. (Klim is "milk" spelled backward and referred to the powdered milk from the Red Cross food parcels that the kriegies used for many things. In other camps, when digging escape tunnels, the klim cans were attached end to end for ventilation pipes. Others put them end to end for stove chimneys. On this march, the cans served as a combination drinking cup and food bowl.)

Slats has no specific memories of days four, five, six, or seven, except that it was becoming harder and harder for some of those around him to keep the pace the guards demanded. And each day, some, because of their slow pace, now caused by blisters that had become septicemic, drifted farther and farther back. Soon, Slats was hearing stories about how the Germans had commandeered some old farm wagons that were now at the end of the columns and carrying kriegies who were sick and with serious foot infections. And, at first, commandeered with the wagons, were old and feeble farm horses that could be spared—animals that sooner or later became exhausted and died. This was good news and bad news. The good news was that there were always kriegies skilled in butchering these unfortunate animals and the boiled meat that was prepared at the next barn was a holiday-type treat for bodies starved for protein. The bad news was that if their incapacitated comrades were going to be moved forward, the kriegies themselves had to band together and assume the role of the draft horse. The fact that many voluntarily took turns doing this is just more evidence that the "band of brothers" concept, so often touted in tales of World War II, was the reality in this dreary stretch of Germany's Pomerania.

Slats feels certain it was their eighth day on the march when a hard rain began falling, an event which turned the already muddy country roads into a quagmire. Walking became more difficult when a shuffling walk—the kind that tired kriegies used to conserve energy—had to become a series of step, lift your foot, throw your leg forward, repeat, calorie-intensive motions that quickly tired even robust physical types like Slats. Undoubtedly, the line of marchers lengthened considerably on this rainy day, but this was just the opening paragraph in a bad-news story. That evening they did not reach a barn—at least the group Slats was with did not. Instead, they were ordered to move into a farmer's pasture, where they were to bed down on the waterlogged turf. And when three or four got together to share their blankets, no one wanted to volunteer their blanket for ground cover because it would just get saturated. They reasoned that, since it would do nobody any

*Descent into the Fifth Circle*

good, and because they were going to get wet anyway, they should lie down on the soaked ground and use their blankets for top cover. But later that evening, a situation that seemingly could not get worse did get worse, because it started to snow. And it was a heavy wet snow that, before the night was over, accumulated to a depth of one to two feet—numbers varying with different accounts, with Slats's memory telling him that it was a lot closer to two feet. And besides the trauma that sharpened his memory of that morning, he insists that, because of the special date, February 14—beside being Valentine's Day, it was also his sister, Hazel's, thirty-first birthday and he felt a special devotion for his only sister—his memory of this particular Wednesday was more acute than the memories of others who have given accounts of that day.

When they began their trek that day in the fresh snow, their motions could be described as a trudge, movements that were as energy sapping as the mud slogging the day before. Then, as the snow was beaten down and mixed with the mud, they again had to return to the equally tiring "step, lift your foot, throw your leg forward" motions. And, once February 14 passed, Slats has no way of accounting for the days that followed. All he can recall is the steady worsening of his physical condition and the constant anxiety of not knowing when or where this trek was going to end.

## CHAPTER 16

## Man as Animal

Another kriegie on the Black March (also known to some as the Death March, the Black Bread March, and the Long March), Russell "Rusty" Harvey from Lebanon, Pennsylvania, wrote a short piece about his thirty-fifth day on the march—a piece that Slats feels strongly mirrors his own sentiments at that time. Here are the first two paragraphs:

> March 12, 1945—I sat in silent solitude and stared at my reflection in a dirty, ice-encrusted pool of water, filled by the melting snow. From my roadside resting place, I saw my face for the first time in thirty-five days. I saw a harried, starved, unshaven, and unbathed skeleton that once walked with pride and dignity as my companions. I now walked with animals, like myself, as companions. I now urinate and defecate in the woods, like an animal, with nothing more to wipe with but a leaf, some straw, or my hand. I now urinate in the streets of small towns like a dog.
>
> I questioned the reason as to why I was here. I stared into the icy pool and I asked, "Why am I here?" "Why me?"

I saw in my icy pool the result of a human that was subjected to the rigors of war who had to submit forcibly to the indignities that only man can force upon another man. My icy pool cast a visual reflection of my countenance; least to say, my icy pool did not reflect my mental attitude. I finally realized that the thin, pale, wild-eyed creatures that were passing by me with death-like expressions were my real reflections; I had two thousand mirrors; I had two thousand reflections. I no longer needed my icy pool to reflect my degradation.

By the first of March, the kriegies had been on the road for twenty-three days and the word of their plight had somehow gotten to the Allied authorities. Undoubtedly, the fighter pilots that now ranged widely over Germany with the license to kill anything that moves almost surely knew to look for a mass of kettle helmets before firing into a column of marching men. At least, Slats cannot remember any of them firing even though, by this time, they were not an uncommon sight. Also, the news of their pathetic condition was released in New York by the Red Cross in the form of a sad warning to the kriegies' loved ones. Here is an excerpt: "Richard F. Allen, Vice-Chairman of the American National Red Cross, says that American prisoners of war in Germany are being marched deeper into the Reich through temperatures as low as thirty degrees below zero without proper clothing. Allen, in charge of insular and foreign operations for the Red Cross, told members of the organization's Brooklyn branch yesterday that 'those of you who have someone in German prison camps must be ready for bad news. . . . I am sorry to tell you that with the structure of Germany breaking up, there is real cause for concern for our prisoners of war.'"

By the time Slats had been on the road a month, the ills that had earlier plagued his fellow marchers now fell upon him. With no further knowledge of the dates of these happenings, he thinks it was sometime in March when he succumbed to the dysentery bacteria that had plagued many at the start. "All I can say is that, especially after you've had a little something to eat, that you just have this powerful urge to go, and then five minutes later, it comes again, and this continues until there is nothing left to squirt. And, at first, I tried to drop my pants out of sight of houses and people, but as my control got worse, I didn't have any choice. Also, I felt terribly ashamed of myself when I couldn't even get my pants down in time. But I wasn't alone. That was happening to people all around me."

The lice also got worse, but, as the weather began to warm up a bit, kriegies, when they got to their barn, went to the lee side out of the wind, stripped off their shirts and began catching the "little gray bastards" and crushing them between their thumbnails. Also, they searched along the seams of their clothing for the strings of tiny white eggs that had been laid. Some, including Slats, were sometimes able to kill them by carefully touching them with the flame of a match. Others used lighted cigarettes for the same purpose. Still others were able to meticulously pick them up and crunch them between their nails. Slats, while engaging in this "kill the little bastards ritual" said that one or more of the kriegies would always chant a regular refrain: *Kill one of the little bastards and a thousand will come to his funeral.*

Once the guards forced them inside their barn, it was another kind of hell for those with dysentery—which was virtually everybody after a while. *"Posten, schitzen!"* became the cry of hundreds who, when finally allowed to exit into the darkened outdoors, felt their way to their right or left of

*Man as Animal*

the barn, always keeping within an arm's length, then while carefully taking one small step backward, squatted, relieved themselves, then came back into the dark barn. But then the difficult task began. Some groups of kriegies say that they were never allowed to walk through the bodies on the floor nor wear their shoes; that they had to crawl with their shoes tied together and hanging from their neck. Slats never experienced those rules. "I wouldn't have taken off my shoes for anybody," he declared. "What we did was prohibit the guys from taking steps. When we had to go, we'd yell *'Posten, schitzen!'* then when we got permission, we would always shuffle our feet—we would never lift them off the floor. That way, if you did hit somebody, it wouldn't hurt like it would if you stepped on them."

Slats got lucky and did not have to suffer some of the horrible nights that others have described. For example, as strung out as the marchers were, groups of kriegies would have to stay in barns where others had slept one or two nights before. And these poor unfortunates often had to sleep on straw contaminated with feces from previous inhabitants who had no way of controlling their bowels long enough to get a guard's attention and shuffle through the crowd on the floor. "Yeah, I was lucky in that respect," Slats said, "but let me tell you, if you had to bed down next to a wall where they had shit outside, the smell would almost make you puke."

It was important for the author to try and corroborate accounts of this Black March when, like Slats, practically all of them were given many years after the event. That is one reason why testimony from such credible witnesses as Dr. Leslie Caplan that was given in Minneapolis on December 31, 1947, is so valuable. Here is what he had to say about diseases in general and dysentery in particular in one of the hearings conducted by those investigating war crimes:

It was common for men to drag themselves along in spite of intense suffering. Many men marched along with large abscesses on their feet or frostbite of extremities. Many others marched with temperatures as high as 105 degrees Fahrenheit. I personally slept with men suffering from erysipelas, diphtheria, pneumonia, malaria, dysentery, and other diseases. The most common disease was dysentery, for this was an inevitable consequence of the filth we lived in and the unsanitary water we drank. This was so common and so severe that all ordinary rules of decency were meaningless. Hundreds of men on this march suffered so severely from dysentery that they lost control of their bowel movements because of severe cramps and soiled themselves. Wherever our column went, there was a trail of bloody movements and discarded underwear (which was sorely needed for warmth). At times the Germans gave us a few small farm wagons to carry our sick. The most these wagons ever accommodated was thirty-five men, but we had hundreds of men on the verge of collapse. It was our practice to load the wagon. As a man would collapse, he would be put on the wagon and some sick man on the wagon would be taken off the wagon to make his way with his exhausted comrades. . . . I do not know what happened to most of the sick men that were left at various places along the march.

Some of the survivors of the march have claimed that when a kriegie collapsed by the side of the road, a guard could be seen waiting until the column was out of sight and then a shot would be heard. We have many testimonies of these kinds of acts from survivors of the infamous Bataan Death March after the Philippines were defeated by the Japanese, but such comparisons with this march have to be labeled as "uncorroborated" or "unauthenticated." However, as other

*Man as Animal*

German atrocities were rampant and have been thoroughly documented, such vile Big Stoop–type behavior may indeed have occurred.

As the days of March passed and the bitterly cruel winter moved past the spring equinox, the days softened and grew longer, meaning that following the late afternoon barn arrival—Slats insists that the group he was with, except for the snowy night of February 14, spent every night in some kind of barn—the kriegies were allowed to sit outside for two or three hours before lockup. Some used this time to take "spit" baths at the farmer's pump, while others continued their war against the "little gray bastards." Slats was sure that was uppermost in his efforts because he hated them so much.

The warm days also created a major new problem that almost caused this twenty-one-year-old Fargo, North Dakota, man's death.

## CHAPTER 17

## The Decision

Food, or the lack of it, became more and more of a problem for the kriegies on the Black March. Red Cross food parcels, which they were occasionally given during the first month of their travel, were not to be seen after that. Their guards claimed that it was the fault of their friends who were bombing and strafing the trains carrying them. The kriegies understood that this could be a part of the problem, but they had also seen guards at Stalag Luft IV ravenously tearing into parcels meant for them and suspected that German officers were commandeering the shipments and diverting them to their own hungry soldiers. And in addition to their aching stomachs creating hunger agony, all the kriegies had to do was look around when they took off their shirts at the end of the day's march and see the devastation that was occurring to their bodies. Rib bones were clearly showing, collar bones were prominent, and elbows looked enlarged when compared to the upper arm where biceps and triceps muscles had atrophied. Slats Slayton estimates that by late March his own weight was getting close to a hundred pounds.

It was also about this time in the march that his food angst came close to getting him in serious trouble. It was one of the days when even the guards agreed that the barn they were to use for the night's lodging was too small for the group under their control. So, through one of the German-speaking kriegies, the guard in charge told them that if some of them would march for another hour or two, they would be rewarded with three potatoes instead of the one potato they would get at the present location. Slats and many others readily agreed that it would be worth it and they set off down the road. And they walked and walked—Slats thinks for more than two hours and maybe closer to three hours; as darkness was coming, they were escorted to another barn. Eagerly, they drank from the farmer's well, then stripped down and began their war against the little gray bastards, talking all the time about how great those potatoes were going to taste—they could see the German guards working at a couple of big boilers and knew they were cooking the potatoes they had promised. But, after they were called to get their food, and after Slats had waited, ravenously hungry, the guard gave him his issue. "But, I'll be a son-of-a-bitch, there was one good potato and the other two were just mush. I rarely get angry, but this just pissed me off to the point where I had to restrain myself to keep from smacking that guy right in the face with those two pieces of crap. God, I was mad, so I quickly walked away just to keep from hitting that guy and getting shot—maybe they wouldn't have done that, but it would have been bad for me. But that just goes to show you how desperate we were by this time."

Slats also had another poignant story to tell about his agonizing hunger. They were trekking through a small village one day and he remembers that his strength was waning and that, because their column was so strung out, there were times when not even a single guard would be in sight. Trudging along, with his head down, out of the corner of his eye he saw a woman coming toward him and she was carrying eggs in both her hands. This, of course, was like seeing huge nuggets of gold, and he quickly called up his little knowledge of German and said something like, *"Do haben zie eir fur siffe"*—his way of asking her if she would trade eggs for soap. Her reply: *"Ya, ya."* So she came over, handed him three eggs and he handed her a half bar of Ivory soap, then, to his surprise, she handed him the three eggs that she had in her other hand. *"Danke, danke, danke,"* he is sure he replied, but as he turned to resume the march, "a Messerschmitt came bearing down on us and we all dove for cover. So there I was, skidding on my face and belly, trying to hold on to those eggs, but it didn't fire on us. Quickly, I picked up the one egg I dropped—it didn't break—stood up and started walking, but I quickly cracked one against my forehead, then gobbled it down, tossed the shell, and cracked another one. I'll bet I swallowed those six eggs in six minutes."

Now the days were getting warmer and the great coat became a shoulder burden along with the head scarf and blanket, which were still needed for night covers. Also, the body pangs did a subtle shift. There was still the stomach agony, signals hammering his brain constantly to find food, find food, find food. But as the temperatures rose, the signals from his parched organs began drowning out those from the stomach. Soon, when the only water they ever got was in the mornings before they left their barn, and in the evenings when they arrived at their new quarters, their real troubles began. What he learned was that, in the warm temperatures that were now upon them, the thirst signals became at least twice as bad as those demanding food. And one only needs to have read any accounts of armed service personnel adrift on rafts in the South Pacific for a period of time to appreciate the strength of this agony. Yes, they knew—they had heard it many, many times—do not drink the seawater because you will die. Yes, you heard that right, do not drink the seawater because your death will come immediately. But what did the men do, though they knew full well they were committing suicide? Some drank the seawater. Why? Did they want to commit suicide? Probably not. It was the overpowering need for water that overwhelmed their minds and literally destroyed their conscious power to resist. And so it was with the kriegies on this Black March. But were they warned? Were they aware of the danger of drinking water from roadside ponds and creeks? Here is one kriegie's story, and it involves Dr. Leslie Caplan:

> The bitter cold and freezing rain was behind us. We were now marching with our GI overcoats over our shoulders. A different form of hardship was upon us—thirst. At least with the snow we could quench our thirst while marching, but without the snow, we would have to endure a waterless march. Water was available at the barn in the morning but without closed containers for carrying water, we could not drink until we arrived that evening at another barn. Several times we passed small streams and some of the POWs broke out of the column and drank water from a stream. Capt. Leslie Caplan, our doctor, reprimanded those guys to the extent that they probably can still hear his tirade today, although he is deceased. I was nearby when Captain Caplan physically dragged one guy from the stream back to the column. He told that POW and the rest of the column that he had been pleading with the commandant for medical supplies for the sick and had been refused, and now if the commandant had learned that POWs were drinking [unsafe] water there would

be no chance at all to convince the commandant of the necessity for medical supplies.

Slats was never with Dr. Caplan on the march, but he now readily admits that he had been warned about the danger of drinking from roadside streams. "I knew what the cows and the pigs did in it, but one day I just couldn't control myself—until you have experienced the kind of thirst we felt—I mean, after walking miles and miles, your body just goes crazy and overrules your brain. Anyhow, we were going by this creek that ran alongside the road and I just went down, took a hand, and scraped back the scum, then, with my klim can, scooped up the water and guzzled it. And even with the horrible taste, you can't know how good that felt just to get water into my body."

It did not take long for the bacteria in that water to do their job on the lining of his intestine. It was almost like the water went straight through him. The problem was that he already had dysentery and after eating almost anything, it was not long before he would have to "drop my drawers" and let the undigested solids exit his body. But now, with this polluted water exacerbating the intestinal irritation, the severe cramps and rumbling gut would not give him the normal reprieve that he had experienced with the lesser form of diarrhea. It was now draining water from his tissues, water that was critical to basic organ function. "Yeah, others had it too, and at night we burned sticks, made charcoal, and a bunch had been chewing and eating it. All the time when they were doing that, I almost wanted to puke and tried not to watch what they were doing. But, this one evening, when we got to our barn, I was right in there with them. I'd take a bit off one of the sticks, pull off a chunk of black stuff with my teeth, then chew and grind and force myself to swallow.

Talk about descending to an animal level. That's when I really felt like I had become an animal."

Slats thinks the charcoal may have helped, but then something worse started happening. One day, on the march, he happened to look at the waste that had exited his body. "And I saw blood. Not dark blood, but bright red blood. That was scary. And it got worse. I hate to tell you this and I dread for my kids to read it. But, as we marched, the urge would come on so sudden that you had no time to drop your pants. You know what I'm saying—I don't want to put it in words. But it was a horrible feeling to be doing this to yourself and it really got me thinking. I never ever, even on that last mission when we were being attacked by all those Focke-Wulfs, thought I was going to die. I don't know what it was, but it was just a strong feeling I had, and I had it all through those months in the hospitals and in those POW camps. But now, knowing that I was losing fresh blood, I also knew that I was slowly losing my life. And as I continued walking and passing blood—I could see it on my shoes—I knew I had to do something and that I couldn't wait much longer. I knew that I had to escape and find some kind of a hospital."

## CHAPTER 18

## Escape and Ecstasy

Two things happened about the same time that Slats Slayton's dysentery worsened. One day their long column marched through the small city of Fallingbostel, which is south of Hamburg and 393.8 road miles from Gross Tychow, where they began the march. The purpose of the Luft IV officers administering the march was to transfer the kriegies to Stalag Luft XIB, which was just outside Fallingbostel. However, when they arrived at the gate, they were denied entrance. After a painful wait outside, they were told that the camp was way too overcrowded and that they would have to turn and head deeper into the Reich. This message was both good and bad. It was good because they interpreted it to mean that the area was about to be overrun by British or American forces. It was bad for obvious reasons: almost all of them were in various kinds of trouble physically, and morale-wise it was a devastating mental blow. However, with new guards under command of Luft XIB, they began retracing their steps.

Then, sometime later, came another blow with an announcement from a guard: *"Roosevelt kaput!"* "That hurt us," Slats said, "because most of us had heard that Truman was just a pawn for the corrupt Pendergast gang in Kansas City. None of us felt that he would be the strong leader that FDR was; he was just a hat salesman that had become a politician. Yeah, we knew the war would go on, but we just hoped that Truman wouldn't do anything as the new commander to slow down Ike."

Franklin D. Roosevelt died on April 12, and right after that Slats really began planning his escape. "After a few days of this [marching in another direction], I was literally squirting blood and knew I didn't have long to live. I knew I had to do something. Then one evening I was outside our barn and looking around and this other guy came up to me, looking like he understood what I was thinking. So I said something or he said something—I can't remember who brought it up—but we started talking about escaping. I know he said, 'If you decide to go, I want to go with you.' And I said, 'That wouldn't be right; I'd just be a liability to you because I'm really sick.' But he persisted. He said that he didn't care and that he would help me. His name was Ray Busiahn and he was from Wood Lake, Minnesota."

Slats thinks it may have been the next day when he fell back in his group, thinking that if he could get on the sick wagon, he might be able to survive without running the risk of escaping. But after he got back there and saw the crowd of sick and lame men clinging to the wagon but unable to ride, he forged ahead, determined that it was escape or die, and he did not want the latter. Finding his new friend, Ray, again, they were walking through a forested area when the one guard supervising his group went down into a deep ditch to relieve himself. Slats realized, when this happened, that it was now or never, and after motioning for Ray to follow him, he hustled off toward the trees on the opposite side of the road. Then he realized that Ray was not following him, so he turned and yelled at him. "Come on," he remembers yelling, even though he was aware that the guard might hear him. Ray then ran toward him and they both vanished into the woods. Slats does not remember how long they walked, but in his condition, he concedes that it could not have been far when they heard guards and a dog coming. At that same time, another escapee, known as Lucky, who had been in Slats's combine at the beginning of the march, saw them, then headed in another direction. Ray and Slats immediately dashed to a pile of branches and leaves, covered themselves as best they could, and waited as the guards headed in the direction Lucky had taken. Slats thinks they might have waited as long as an hour to make sure the guards were not around before they uncovered themselves and started walking. "I was a mess, I mean a real mess, and by now I could barely walk, and I told Ray that he had to be the guide, that I couldn't even think about which direction to go. Actually, I think I was as close to dying as I have ever been. I could almost see it coming. But Ray literally saved my life. He was patient, he walked at my pace, and he kept encouraging me while I stumbled through the trees.

"And then we met three Russians and they were in a little clearing and had potatoes that they were boiling. I'm sure I looked like a starving animal as I stared at those potatoes, but then I realized how I had lucked out meeting Ray. He was German and spoke the language fluently—and these Russians, who had probably been slave laborers working for Germans for a year or more, could also speak German. Quickly, Ray explained our hunger problem and soon they were handing each of us a potato. Man, they were hot and I'm sure I burned my mouth. But I couldn't wait; I had to get that sucker in my belly, so like a hungry pig, I devoured it. The Russians were

*Escape and Ecstasy*

getting quite a kick out of seeing the way I acted, and soon they were handing me another. I let this one cool a bit, but then scarfed it down. 'Do you want another one?' Ray asked. The Russians were still smiling and enjoying my performance, but I couldn't resist. I said, 'Hell, yes, I can eat another one.'

They spent that night, which was April 16, with the Russians, then the two of them started walking the next morning with the potatoes they were given. Slats insists that he was not fully alert as they walked, depending completely upon Ray to guide him in a logical direction, and that the physical act of walking was the most severe physical challenge he has ever experienced. But he also noticed something else, although he admits that it could have been imagination. What he thinks he noticed was a decline in the blood flow from his rectum. "It seemed like it was less whether it actually was or not, and if it was less, it could have been because of those potatoes I ate—I also ate one before we started walking."

Slats thinks they headed south and is certain that they lucked out having continuing mild spring weather. They camped somewhere in a forest the next night, and the next morning, while Ray was building a fire and preparing to boil two of their precious potatoes, Slats remembers hearing a rumbling noise, and it seemed to be about a hundred yards away. Immediately, he started sneaking through the trees—he did not want to stumble into a German armed column—and to his utter surprise, he saw an American tank and a soldier standing up and looking out of the hatch. He went through the trees as rapidly as he could move, and when he got closer, he realized that it was, indeed, an American tank, but that it had the British insignia on it. Of course, at that point, he could have cared less; he immediately walked out into the road, causing the tank to stop. "You a POW?" the guy in the tank yelled down at him.

"I sure am," was the answer Slats thinks he gave him.

"Well, look out," the tanker said, and he reached down, was handed a tin container "about fourteen inches tall from one of the guys in the tank," and threw it out toward Slats. Meanwhile, a whole string of tanks were coming from behind the lead tank, and it also started to move forward. Slats doesn't remember if the tanker yelled anything else to him, but he clearly remembers grabbing the tin from the ground and, despite his infirmity, "almost running back to where Ray was building the fire. When I got there, I kicked over the little pot he had and said, "Come on, we don't need these spuds, let's get our ass out of here—we've been liberated, there's British tanks out there."

When they got back to the road, the first thing they did was open the tin and began gorging on the food that was in there. Slats remembers that it was more than half full, and he is sure that he and Ray had consumed most of it when, suddenly, they began retching and continued retching until "we barfed up everything we had eaten." It was just about then, Slats remembers, when they heard the sound of another motor vehicle coming down the road. As they waited, now sure that it would be a friendly Brit, a weapons carrier came into view with just one soldier in it, and it stopped when it reached them. "I still remember that guy's name: it was Sergeant Adams and he was one of the nicest guys you could meet. Not only did he introduce himself, but he went on to explain that one of his orders was to look for escapees like us and help them. After he explained that, he said, 'And I'm carrying pencils and stationery just so guys like you can write a letter home and let your families know that you're now safe.' Then he handed us paper and pencil and we immediately sat down by the side of the road and wrote our families—I still have the letter that I wrote to my mother that day. Anyhow, we handed him the

*Escape and Ecstasy*

letters, he sealed them in an envelope, and we each wrote our home address on them and gave them back. Talk about a relief. I'm sure I was a hundred percent better."

Slats was then asked to try and use one word to describe what it was like to know that he was free and safe. He declined to answer for a day or two, then, one morning, he said, "By the way, you asked for one word describing how I felt when we were liberated. Well, I visited my Webster's and came up with this word: ecstasy, a state of overwhelming emotion, rapturous delight." Then he added, "You know, there is no word that can come close to really describing the actual feeling I had, but that's the best I could come up with."

## CHAPTER 19

The Doctors Take Over

Slats Slayton can remember a British truck with a canvas cover picking his new friend, Ray Busiahn, and him up "somewhere in a forested area," where the driver helped him into the back. And because he has no memory of the ride, he thinks there was a good chance that he went to sleep immediately. What he does remember is that it probably lasted about an hour and that they ended up at a British facility in the German city of Celle.

There, he does clearly remember them telling him, while still outside, to strip out of his feces-stiffened pants and other clothes and stack them so they could be burned without anybody having to touch them. Then, naked, he went through a delousing chamber and was then escorted to a shower where "I am sure this had to be one of the most pleasant moments of my life. It was just ecstasy standing in there, soaking up that hot water." When reminded that this was the second time he had used that descriptive word, he retorted, "I don't care; it was ecstasy, both the hot water and the knowledge that I was clean again! Stop and think, I had walked for seventy days and I really never had a chance to be completely clean for months before that. Just think of the joy of soaping up and feeling that hot water against my back. I think I could have stood in that shower for a week. No, that's an exaggeration. I don't want to exaggerate, I want people to know the truth. But, the truth is, and I'll repeat it, that shower was one of the most pleasant experiences of my life."

After the shower, a male attendant examined his hair and led him to the delousing chamber again. After that, he took another shower, was given some underclothes to wear, then was taken to a room where they cut his hair and shaved him. Then, he was examined by a doctor and does not remember much after that because "I was so weak, I probably passed out—at least, I don't remember taking any medication, although I'm sure they gave me some."

What he does remember is that they gave him a British uniform and shoes to wear, that he slept for "quite a while," and that they took Ray and him to an airport, helped him board a Short Sterling bomber, and flew them to Brussels. There, they were taken to a Lancaster bomber and flown by the Royal Canadian Air Force to Oxford, England, where there was a hospital run by American medical personnel.

Once there, "all I can remember is that Ray went along with me, and then, when I got to that hospital, they deloused me again and then they put me to bed. Also, I can remember that I became extremely dizzy whenever I tried to stand up. But that's all. I went completely blank and found out later what happened:

> I woke up and opened my eyes. I was looking at a ceiling. I was not in a barn; I was in a room, a clean room. I must have laid there awhile, trying to get my bearings. Then I heard a noise out in the hall. Somebody said the word "donutmobile."

I think I probably began salivating. Just the thought of eating a donut—I simply can't describe it. But it was a powerful urge and I swung my feet over the side of the bed and, leaning on the bed, tried to stand up, and I became extremely dizzy until I was up for a while. And then I started to worry. Was the donutmobile going to leave? I forced myself up and remember staggering to the door, then to where this lady was handing out donuts and coffee. I didn't want the coffee, but she handed me the most beautiful glazed donut I had ever seen.

But, about then, this guy comes up to me and says rather curtly, "What are you doing out of bed?" I looked right at him and said, "What the hell do you think I'm doing—I'm getting a donut, and what business is it of yours?" Then his expression softened and he said, in a friendly tone, "I'm your doctor and you should be back in that bed." I felt terrible for the way I barked at him and tried to apologize. But he smiled and said, "Go ahead and eat your donut; then go back to bed; I'll be in in a few minutes and check you out and talk to you. So, I wolfed down that donut, got back in bed, propped myself up with the pillow, and waited.

Then he came in with a nurse and started talking to me. He said that I had been in a coma for thirty-six hours and that they had been worried that I would not wake up. Then he went on to explain some things that I've forgotten, but I think he may have said that I was severely dehydrated and that they had given me blood and maybe blood plasma, and I know he said that they had given me some kind of antibiotic shots. But what I remember most is the part about never waking up. That got to me. Oh, yeah, and he also told me about my temperature. He said that for all that time it had been 105 degrees and I had sweat so much they had to change my mattress. He also said that he had been afraid I would have

*The Doctors Take Over*

some brain damage from that long period of high temperature. But then he said that when I came back at him while out in the hall, he was glad that I did that because it told him that my brain was okay—that I would have been mumbling and stumbling if I had suffered brain damage. He also said that, with my temperature that high for so long, I couldn't have a live germ left in my body—that the heat would have killed them all.

And, boy, did I feel better after hearing all that. When they left, all I could think about was that I was going to have a life. And that thought probably stayed in my mind. I was going to live, I was going to go home and do all the things that I didn't dare think about when I was a POW. That's when I really realized that my war was finally over.

One of the next things Slats remembers is them putting him on a scales and weighing him. "I weighed 104 pounds and they think I probably had gotten down to 98 before I started eating those potatoes and the food the Brits had given me. I think I probably weighed about 155 when we went on that last mission, so what's that, 57 pounds I probably lost? But, man, the way I was eating now, I was sure going to get it back."

However, there was an additional problem. The doctor explained to him that he was suffering from jaundice, which turns the eye whites and the skin yellow—unless the skin is naturally dark or tanned. Because Slats's jaundice was mild, he just needed to stick to a special diet that eliminated meat products. During the immediate future, at least, he was ordered to eat only starchy foods.

Every day he was brought four or five small meals and urged to eat as much as he could. "Ray spent a lot of time in the room with me—I think, when we were still in Germany, that I must have told them he had saved me by helping me escape and that I needed him with me, otherwise, since he was healthy, I think they would have shipped him directly to Lucky Strike, the camp in Le Havre, France, where—I found this out in Oxford—they were taking all of the ex-POWs that had been released. But they let him sleep somewhere in that hospital and I guess he was under some kind of orders to stick with me. Anyhow, he would sit there while I stuffed myself, then they would take away the dishes and we'd talk about all kinds of things. I know he loved farming—his parents had a farm outside Wood Lake, Minnesota—and he was anxious to get back and start work on their farm. I'm sure I probably started thinking about what I was going to do with myself back in Fargo when I got there, and maybe talked to him about going to college. Some kind of a counselor, or maybe it was a chaplain—I can't remember—came by to see us and told us about the GI Bill that Roosevelt had gotten passed before he died. Before the war, I never dreamed that I could ever afford to go to college—I don't think many of my generation raised in the Depression ever thought they would go to college. I know, or at least I don't remember any kind of talk like that in the camps. College was strictly for rich folks before the war. But Ray had no interest even if the government was going to pay for all his tuition and books. He wanted to be a farmer, period. I remember him saying that growing things was as much pleasure as he wanted out of life, especially after the months that he had been cooped up in POW camps and the seventy days we spent on the march."

The remainder of Slats's time at Oxford is pretty much a blur, other than the fact that he ate and ate until his stomach began to stretch, and that, within a few days, he could tell that his stomach was beginning to adapt to food. The dizzy spells went away, he could get in and out of his bed without any problems, and he was beginning to enjoy walking in the hall, especially knowing the more he walked, the stronger he was going to get. Then the magic day came when they told him two things. Staff Sergeant Slayton, you are now well enough to be released on your own from this hospital; however, you must stay on the high-starch, no-meat diet until a doctor tells you otherwise. Also, Sergeant Slayton, we are giving you orders to go to London, where you will be transported to a ship that will take you home.

That very good news had to be ringing in his ears as Slats and his guide emerged from their inferno. Dante, when he did that, said, "My guide and I . . . saw, through a round opening, some . . . things of beauty. . . . It was from there that we emerged, to see—once more—the stars." Had Slats known of Dante's journey and felt the need to describe his own emergence, in the raw GI language he was using at the time, he might have said about his own guide, "Thank God for Ray—if he hadn't helped me escape, I would have been dead had I tried to walk the additional sixteen days the others did before they were liberated. He truly saved my ass, and even though England is always cloudy, we were out in the sun again."

## CHAPTER 20

# Going Home

*Going home, going home, I'm just going home. . . .*

Antonín Dvořák's ninth "New World" symphony was first performed on December 16, 1893, in Carnegie Hall. Not long after that one of the melodies in that symphony was used for the popular song "Going Home." The author was curious if the poignancy of the words in the song could have been in Slats's mind when he learned that he was to be released from the Oxford Hospital and was being sent home—it was commonly sung when the author was in elementary school. To test this, the author asked Slats's wife if she could be playing a few bars on her organ some day when Slats was coming in the door from doing an errand. She agreed, and when she heard his car arrive after he had been to the post office, she started playing it. Shortly afterward, the author's telephone rung, and the first thing he heard was Slats singing the words of the song. Answer to the question: absolutely, both the words and the melody were in his mind. "What a beautiful, beautiful song," he said. Clearly, the words and the melody were indicative of his mood, his thoughts, and his feelings when, after his bout with dehydration and severe dysentery, he would see his home again. And now, there would be no pain and no stumbling, and his mother would be waiting.

They went by train from Oxford to London. It was Ray Busi-ahn, a sergeant with the last name of Jablonski, another sergeant whose name Slats has forgotten, and himself, now in his new dress uniform with his pants' waist tucked under for two or three inches and his buttoned collar hanging open by at least an inch. "You'll grow into 'em young man," he thinks the elderly supply sergeant may have said when he handed Slats the uniform that matched his original size.

When they got off the train, boarded an open truck, and began their trek to the Hans Crescent Club, Slats could not have cared less how his uniform drooped on his scraggly frame. It was the crowd that the truck crept through that had all of their attention. Hoards of people were gathered for a victory parade, and soon the crowd had to make way for their truck and vehicles coming from the other direction. And in that first vehicle, which had an open top, Prime Minister Winston Churchill was standing, waving to the crowd and holding his fingers in a "V" with both hands while he held "a big cigar in his mouth." It was jubilation and ecstasy all over again, but it was no longer a private matter for Slats; it was being shared by thousands who were now free from the fear of buzz bombs and v-2 rockets, and thousands of others who now knew their loved ones were safe and would soon be home. Slats has no idea what day in May this was, whether it was the official VE (Victory in Europe) Day, May 8, 1945, or a premature celebration. What he is certain of is that, by the time they checked into their quarters, there was not a drop of beer or booze available in all of London; everything purchasable in any kind of retail establishment, including all the pubs, had been consumed. The Londoners, in short, were literally drunk with excitement.

But they need not have worried. It just so happened that Staff Sergeant Jablonski had a good friend who lived in an area of north London called Crouch End, which was (and still is) home to many "creative types." "I'll call him," Jablonski said. "He was in the British Navy but got an early discharge for something physical, and I know he'll have plenty to drink." So Jablonski did that, they took the Tube to his friend's neighborhood, found his home, and were welcomed by the friend, his wife, and their two kids. Then, from his ample stock of beer and liquor, they partied "for at least forty-eight hours." Feeling guilty because they had not checked the bulletin board at their quarters as they were supposed to do each day, they decided to quit the party. However, to return their hosts' hospitality, and to give them a special treat since they had been living on very restrictive diets because of many years of tight rationing, they invited them to the Hans Crescent Club, where they were assured that great food was plentiful twenty-four hours a day.

The family joined them and Slats still chuckles when he recalls the look on their two kids' faces when they saw the canned peaches in the cafeteria line of food. "That's all they would eat," he says. "I mean, they hadn't had canned peaches for years and they couldn't get enough. We really enjoyed seeing those kids eat, and before they left we got a couple of cans for our hosts and stuffed the kids' pockets with candy." And although Slats did not say it, he and his friends, while watching those kids wolf down the peaches, probably thought of what it would have been like for them to have come on food like that just a few weeks earlier.

Slats thinks it was a short time later when they received orders to report to a truck that hauled them to Southampton, where they boarded a ship his memory says was the *General Butler* and went to Le Havre, where hundreds of ex-

POWs joined them on board. Then, it was down the Channel and out into the Atlantic, where Slats remembers two things happening. First, he had the pleasure of stumbling into his old crewmate, Walt Abernathy from Tupelo, Mississippi. In conversations with the former waist gunner and fellow POW, Slats heard again how, on their last mission, Abernathy had looked through the tail-wheel passage and then reported to their pilot, Fridgen, that Slats was slumped over his armor and unconscious—and act that ended up saving his life. They also discussed their respective experiences in Luft VI and Luft IV, and their separate but similar treks across Germany. Slats remembers that Abernathy survived the entire eighty-six-day Black March and was well enough at liberation to be sent directly to Camp Lucky Strike.

Slats's second vivid memory is being awakened one night and told that he should get up to the top deck. He did this and could hardly believe what he was seeing. During previous nights when he looked out from the top deck, he could see nothing; there were no lights visible anywhere and he could not see any other ships in the convoy. But this night when he went up, lights were ablaze and he could clearly see what he thinks he remembers as the other seven or eight ships in their convoy. "It was the prettiest sight I've ever seen; it was like a small city with all those lights. We were told that the Atlantic has just been declared neutral territorial water, now safe from German submarines. What a sight! Talk about an escape to freedom. There it was, like a big painting, all lit up for us."

Slats then described the end of the voyage and the sight that every returning veteran from Europe also vividly remembers. That, of course, was the Statue of Liberty, the one symbol for which they had put their lives on the line. Slats said, "For me, it was a big deal, no doubt about that, but it was just one more good thing that was happening in my life. But it still couldn't compare to what I experienced when I saw that first British tank."

His next memory is very poignant. After they disembarked and took the train to Camp Dix (now Fort Dix) in New Jersey, he remembers an officer getting up in front of all them and saying, "Welcome home, fellas. And to make your homecoming something special, each of you is going to be given the biggest steak you have ever seen in your life. I guarantee that none of you will be able to eat it all." This, of course, was a painful thing for Slats to hear, because "I couldn't even eat a bite of it; I had to have potatoes and macaroni and cheese and things like that. But I took one anyhow and shared it with Ray and some of the other guys sitting around me. For sure, they all tried to prove that major wrong, and it didn't go to waste."

After a long reprocessing session—Slats does not remember how long except that it was long for all the guys dying to start on their way home—he was put in charge of three others, including his friend, Ray, and that he was ordered to make certain that his charges would not leave his supervision until they reached Fort Snelling outside Minneapolis. "I only had trouble with one guy. He was kind of a smartass and when we got to Chicago, he said 'so long' and that, whether I liked it or not, he had a girlfriend there and he was going to see her. I simply told him that this was fine if he wanted to do it, but that it was my duty to report him and that I sure as hell intended to follow my orders. Bitching like hell, he sat back down and I didn't hear anything more out of him for the rest of the trip."

When they reached Minneapolis and Fort Snelling, Slats went through more processing and another physical exam, after which he was free to go on a normal diet, and then he was issued a complete supply of clothes and other standard

GI items. He also collected all of his back pay, which, for fifteen months, was a total of $2,592.00 after deducting the $18.75/month he had authorized for War Savings Bonds that he had arranged to have sent to his mother, bonds which, ten years after they were purchased, would be worth $25 each. He also received orders at this time placing him on sixty-four days of temporary duty (TDY) that he was to spend at home. Then, after being released, he and Ray honored a pact that they had agreed on back when they were still on the Black March. "We said then, that if we ever got out of this thing alive, that we were going to meet somewhere and really tie one on. Well, this was the time to do it, so we went to the Nicollet hotel, the swankiest hotel in Minneapolis, and did we ever party. I remember it was the Jolly Miller Bar downstairs and did we ever get loaded—two bellhops had to help us up to our rooms. The next morning, really hung over, I caught a train for Fargo. I had wired my mom from Fort Dix, but I didn't know if she had a phone or not so I didn't try to call her. This was the last time I saw Ray. I tried to contact him a number of years later and found out that he had died at a young age."

The next thing that happened to him he would remember for the remainder of his life.

## CHAPTER 21

The Rest of the Story

Slats Slayton's second daughter, Theresa, told the author the story of what happened when Slats's Northern Pacific train from Minneapolis pulled into the train station in Fargo: "When the train stopped at the station, dad saw his oldest brother, Einer, pacing back and forth on the platform. He said he wondered how Einer could have known that he was arriving, and he soon got the answer. Einer saw him get off the train and rushed to dad, gave him a big hug, then told him how glad he was to see him. Then he explained that for the last two weeks, after their mother had received dad's wire from New Jersey, he had met every train from the east because he didn't want dad to get off the train and not have anybody there to meet him and to welcome him home. Dad told us kids that story several times as we were growing up and every time he told the story, it always brought tears to his eyes."

Einer took Slats to his parents' apartment where he surprised his mother—his dad was working at the time—and Slats says that he will always remember her first exclamation: "Son, you just look wonderful!" The reason why her comment is so memorable for him is that it reminds him of how much weight he had regained since his liberation. "I probably wasn't anywhere near back to 155 pounds, but at least I wasn't that scraggly-looking skeleton I had seen in the mirror at the Oxford Hospital."

Einer left Slats and returned to the Phillips 66 service station he had purchased with money he had earned working in a Seattle shipyard during the war. Then Slats, surely while his mother plied him with much food, heard all the latest family news. He also heard something that disturbed him. His mother, in apologetic tones, explained how his dad had made her sign over all the savings bonds Slats had arranged to have sent her each month, savings that Slats had planned to use while pursuing some postwar training or a career, and savings that his dad later confessed that he "threw away playing poker." However, it was not completely bad news; his dad had taken some of the money and bought a cheap, "well used" 1938 Plymouth that he had been driving to work, but which Slats was now entitled to own.

The next weeks went by rapidly. Slats thinks he was out somewhere every night. First, he went to the Fargo Arena "a couple of times" but did not see anybody at the roller rink that he knew. He also made the rounds of the nightclubs and certain restaurants, and, for later generations to understand what this means, it is necessary to review a bit of history.

In the late forties the country was flooded with millions of single men who had returned home with primarily one thing on their minds: GIRLS, in capital letters. Literally, having gone without female companionship for two, three, four—even five years, they were starved for the kind of affection only the female could provide. At the same time, the country was overloaded with single girls age sixteen to twenty-four who were living in fear that, unless they found a man quickly, they would soon be too old to marry and would end up with a name that was hugely pejorative at the time: Old Maid. The reader has to believe that being called an Old Maid was far, far worse than in today's world where being a mature single woman has no stigma attached. In short, in the years immediately after World War II, there were literally millions of extremely strong opposite-poled magnets loose in the country that had an abnormally strong attraction for each other. And the consequence? After the war, nightclubs with dance facilities and either live bands or the new and highly evolved jukeboxes that played 78 rpm records for a nickel, exploded in number.

And it was not only nightclubs that attracted singles in search of each other. Some restaurants were remodeled with dance floors for young people who often had to be twenty-one before being admitted, and to singles who, for religious or other reasons, did not want to be in an environment where everyone was drinking.

So the twenty-one-year-old young man who just two years earlier was so shy he regularly turned down good-looking girls that wanted to dance with him, now made up this lost time with vengeance. In just weeks he learned to jitterbug, waltz, polka, and schottische, the latter a Bohemian dance imported by several nationalities of European immigrants and often danced to "Cotton-Eyed Joe." And he turned out to be nothing like many of the relatively sedate male dancers that were also learning to dance. As a young man before the war he had reveled in the acrobatic, show-stopping antics he and his friend, Cliff Myhra, had performed at various skating rinks. These same urges were driving him now and he admits that he got great satisfaction out of dance floor performances that caused the other dancers to back off and cheer. "I have to say that I got to be pretty darn good out there," he said, remembering those happy hours he spent dancing on that sixty-four-day TDY.

Slats got bored sitting around his mother's apartment during the day. When Einer got busy or needed time off, Slats, just to have something to do, went to work in the service station, but this created a new problem he had to solve. All of the civilian clothes he had at home were many sizes too small for him. He said, "I looked at a sport coat that I had paid sixteen dollars for—a whole lot of money at the time—and it was just tiny—only a child could wear it." In order to have something other than his uniform to work in, he took one pair of his uniform trousers to a dry cleaning shop and had them dyed green. Then, because it was summertime, he could get by with just those pants and a cheap T-shirt. "So, while I partied almost every night, I worked a lot at Einer's station, but I don't think I did a lot of thinking about what I was going to do with my life. I think I was just enjoying life, living it day to day. I also have to admit that I sometimes partied a little hard and would sometimes say to Einer the next day, 'I had kind of a bad night last night and don't feel too sharp,' and he would say, 'Ah, it's a little slow today, why don't you take the rest of the day off.' I'm telling you this just to point out how close we were and how well we got along together."

The days passed quickly in Fargo and it was soon time to catch a train to Santa Monica, California, where he had orders to report to the Edgewater Beach Club Hotel, a beautiful resort on the Pacific Ocean. "They really didn't want us there," he remembers, "so they sent me to a recovery hospital at Fort Logan just outside of Denver. There, the doctors decided I didn't need any rehabilitation—I just couldn't completely straighten out my right leg—and so they asked me if there was anything I wanted to do. I said that I wouldn't mind playing some golf, so for three straight days they took me to the Cherry Hills Country Club where they rented clubs for me and paid the greens fees. After the third day, they called me in and said that my golf was getting too expensive for their budget and that they were going to discharge me. Then, on September 19, they gave me a CDD, which is a Certificate of Disability Discharge. That discharge gave me a 60 percent disability, partly because I had been a POW and partly because my leg could not be snapped completely open. Then they paid for my travel back to Fargo."

By then it was too late to enroll in college, which he had decided to do since with the GI Bill he could get a $65/month (in 1948 raised to $75/month) stipend along with the payment of his tuition and books. Needing something to do for the rest of the school year, he decided, since they got along so well, that he would spend some of his savings and buy into Einer's service station.

It was after doing Einer's bookkeeping that he began to realize that, if he had any real talent, it was an ability to work with numbers. Looking back, he credited both the ease and pleasure he experienced with Einer's books for convincing him that accounting was a profession he could enjoy. That spring he applied to the prestigious Wharton School of Business in Philadelphia, Pennsylvania. "That turned out to be a bummer. They wrote me back saying the class was full, but then a guy from Fargo whose dad was connected in politics, applied later than me, and even though his grades were not as good as mine, he was accepted." Slats also applied to Denver University, but after waiting what seemed like forever to hear if he was accepted, he decided to just enroll at the University of North Dakota in Grand Forks. Then, two days after he had registered there, he received an acceptance notice from Denver University. "I basically said the hell with it, I'll stay at Grand Forks."

There he was initiated into the Sigma Alpha Epsilon Fraternity and lived in the frat house. He said that he enjoyed most of his college classes and that he got excellent grades in most of them. The following summer he worked with Einer, but then the following year Einer died a premature death. The problem was that he had experienced a ruptured appendix when seven years old and had to be taken a number of miles in a horse-drawn wagon to the hospital. The surgery was only partly successful, and he had ten more surgeries at points during his young life, then he got some kind of intestinal blockage that ended up killing him. "That was real sad for me because he was always my favorite brother. Although he wasn't an outstanding golfer like the other brothers, he was one helluva bowler. He bowled one perfect game and twelve 299 games. He was only thirty-four when he died."

Just before Slats was to begin his senior year, he got a call from his brother Jimmy, who was living in Billings, Montana. He was told that his mother, who had gone there to visit two sisters and Jimmy's family, was in the hospital and in critical condition. Slats immediately caught a train for Billings but arrived too late. She died in the hospital and Slats, because of Jimmy's perpetual money problems, had to pay the first class fare to ship her body home and for all the funeral expenses. His dad, as usual, was also broke, and, consequently, when Slats insisted that her funeral be held in the Catholic Church, which his dad hated, he heard no objections. "That was a good thing," said Slats, "because by then, I'd had enough of my father, and was ready to tie into him if he had objected."

His mother's death and the money he spent caused Slats to reassess his desire to attend college his final year for a degree. He already had the knowledge and skills to work as an accountant. Also, he saw getting credentials as a Certified Public Accountant (CPA) as "something that was just political." These two factors, what he knew he could do and what he knew he did not want to do, convinced him that it was time to drop out of college and start a career, that he was not going to gain anything of value by delaying his entry into the business world for another year. So, while "still down in the dumps because of mom," he decided to go to Billings, live temporarily with his brother Jimmy, and look for a job.

In Billings Slats found a job at International Harvester and almost immediately received a raise when a visiting executive discovered his work, but was soon recruited by two businessmen from Buffalo, Wyoming (who heard about him from a mutual friend), offering him a higher salary. It was in Buffalo that Slats really began to blossom into manhood. He boarded with a wonderful family that took care of him like one of their own, did some outstanding work in two different car dealerships, danced the legs off a number of attractive young women, then married one that he met at a New Year's Eve dance. Her name was Zella and, coincidentally, she, too, had been a war hero. At the beginning of the war, she enlisted in the Women's Army Corps (WACS), went to cryptography school, and while stationed in Tunisia, single-handedly broke one of the German secret codes. Just before their marriage, Slats was enticed by the owner of the First National Bank of Buffalo, a private institution, to join the staff. And while working his way up to assistant manager—he could never have become manager because that position was reserved for family or family designees—he and Zella had four children: David (1956), Paula (1957), Theresa (1959), and Mary (1961).

While working at the bank, Slats became heavily involved in sports and community affairs. He was the catcher on the city's softball team, he was a club champion at the local golf course, was city police judge under two different mayors, was president of the local chamber of commerce, and, when it was a broken organization, almost single-handedly revitalized the Little League baseball team and, in his first year at the helm of that organization, had them completely outfitted in new uniforms.

Slats retired from the bank in 1986, then fulfilled a dream of visiting the farm in Germany where Fridgen crash landed Homing Pigeon. There, he was lucky to find Appelonia Boskum, the woman who as a sixteen-year-old, saw waist gunner Oliver Gaby's parachute fall into a tree after Lieutenant Waller had pushed him out of the airplane. Along with another girl, they managed to extricate him, and Appelonia told Slats how Gaby died while she was holding him in her arms. Slats also went to the hospital in Unna, hoping to thank the doctor who did the good job of extracting the shrapnel from under his kneecap. That was unsuccessful because he had died, but his brother, who was present during the surgery, clearly remembered the incident and was able to fill him in on other details he did not know.

Slats has also received visits and phone calls from radioman Bill Reilly, who went on to become a bartender in Las Vegas; retired Maj. Francis Fridgen, who stayed in service, flew cargo ships during the Berlin airlift, and retired as an Air Force pilot; waist gunner Walt Abernathy; and crew chief Bob Brennan. From them he learned that Lieutenant Palmer's chute failed to open when he bailed out just before the crash landing, and that Lieutenant Waller died when the rear of Homing Pigeon broke off during the landing. Slats also tried to contact his best friend on the crew, Garrett Bartle, but was informed that he had died young of pancreatic cancer. Every Christmas, he receives a card from Abraham Homar, who was with Slats in Luft IV and who suffered a knockdown from the goon called Big Stoop, and Slats's wife,

Zella, regularly talks on the phone with Norma Piere, his barracks' mate Sam Piere's wife.

And Slats at the time of this writing? He just turned eighty-nine. He is out of his house between five thirty and six every morning so he can join a group of locals who gather for coffee and breakfast. Then he tries to stay busy during the day, well aware of the "use it or lose it syndrome." The one downer in his life is that the beginning of macular degeneration in one eye keeps him from any lengthy reading. When asked to describe his life in a sentence or two, he said, "Despite the poverty in my growing-up years and the tough years of the war, I feel that I have had a happy life because I've had the privilege of living with a wonderful, loving wife for fifty-seven years, and because I've had the great pleasure of raising four wonderful children. And what would be the number one thing I'd tell young people today if they asked my advice? I'd say take what comes, no matter what it is, and then make the best of it."